ADVANCE PRAISE FOR
BECOMING ME WHILE RAISING YOU

Becoming Me While Raising You is a compelling story of one woman's journey to find her own authentic voice through life and into motherhood. Kim brings the reader deeply into her world. In order to fully understand herself she looks back at the puzzle pieces of her life that contributed to how she arrived where she is today. Kim shares her unique perspective as a mother of a child with an addiction and how she survived and, in the end, thrived. Through this book, the reader is given insight and understanding into themselves, their belief systems, and the impact those belief systems may be having on their present-day life. Kim offers support and advice along the way through her own example of surviving one of life's hardest challenges. This nonfiction book reads like fiction and I was unable to put it down once I began reading. Kim's book is a must read for anyone who is overwhelmed and looking to find the answers that lie within their very own heart.

Janet Philbin, LCSW, CHt: Author of *Show Up for Yourself- A Guide to Inner Awareness and Growth*

Becoming Me

While Raising You

a mother's journey to her self

KIM MÜENCH

Cover Photo by Bhikku Amitha

Author Photo by Dawn Michelle Photography

Cover and Interior Design by https://BethanyRuth.com

Dedication

I am convinced that life is about seeking your truth. This book is dedicated to mothers everywhere who use their parenting journey as a vehicle to find themselves.

I'd like to deeply thank the following people who have contributed to my uncovering the truth about who I am.

Jenny and Don, thank you for bringing me into the world and for always doing your best to support and nurture me. Choosing you as my mom and dad was perfect!

I am deeply grateful to Tom, my husband of twenty-nine years, who has helped me grow in countless and meaningful ways as a mom, woman, and human being.

And, of course, I want to appreciate the children who have chosen to come into the world through me. Thank you to Nick, Allen-Michael, Brigham, Maddux, Mia, and the one I didn't have the opportunity to meet in this physical life, but whom I know I will surely recognize on the other side.

Some of the names in this book have been changed in order to protect identity, though the circumstances reflect true and actual events.

Contents

Foreword

As far back as I can remember, my mother has been one of the most kind, nurturing, and level-headed individuals I have ever had the good fortune to know. Then again, I might be biased.

A decade ago, she approached me with a question and an idea. She wanted to share the experiences and knowledge that she gained through her own journey on my road to recovery from alcoholism. In some ways it was our recovery as a family. These series of experiences helped act as a conduit for change in her life, laying down the course for a new mission to help others. That took many forms over the years, finally culminating in the decision to help those in need to develop healthy parenting techniques.

My time in treatment helped me become more comfortable in sharing my experience with others and, in general, be a more open and honest person. It doesn't get much more open than having your story shared in a published book! After some thought, I gave her the green light. She got so much out of her experience through me, why not use that to help others?

The following pages contain the story of a woman who has

been through just about anything life can throw her way, both blessings and misfortunes. My own life has taken many twists and turns since the events in this book took place. However, I always make it a point to keep my past experiences, especially the ones detailed in this book, close to my heart. They serve as a reminder of where I came from and where I am now. My mother played a big role in that, and I am forever grateful.

I wouldn't be the man I am today without the strength, courage, determination, and unconditional love from a woman I am proud to call, "Mom." I truly hope the words on the pages that follow resonate and provide guidance in some way on your own journey, and if that ends up taking you to my mother and her practice, then you couldn't be in better hands.

Nick

May 2021

OUR DEEPEST FEAR IS NOT THAT WE ARE INADEQUATE.

OUR DEEPEST FEAR IS THAT WE ARE POWERFUL BEYOND MEASURE.

IT IS OUR LIGHT, NOT OUR DARKNESS, THAT MOST FRIGHTENS US.

Marianne Williamson

Introduction

It didn't happen overnight. My journey to becoming a more awake, aware, conscious, and intentional woman has evolved gradually over the last decade and, quite frankly, I'll always be a work in progress. There have been many ups and downs — moments of confusion, anxiety, and clarity along the way — to be shared in the pages ahead.

My "awakening"/parenting wake-up call/the beginning of my transformation involves a hot, Texas summer afternoon when my daughter Mia was four years old. She is the youngest of five and the baby girl in our family of seven.

Mia was sitting in her usual spot, the back back of our old "silver bullet" minivan. She was wearing her uniform, which at the time was a pink sleeveless dress with a tulle skirt and her beloved fur-lined pink Crocs. As we drove home from dropping off one of her older brothers at yet another baseball practice, Rihanna was playing on the radio, and Mia began to sing enthusiastically along, *"'Cause I may be bad but I'm perfectly good at it / Sex in the air I don't care / I love the smell of it / Sticks and stones may break my bones / but whips and chains excite me."* Like a slap across the face, it hit me that my preschooler knew the words to a song about a topic no four-year-old could or should understand. Yet I knew at the same moment that the message, whether she understood it or not, was being internalized as she listened.

Questionable song lyrics, by Rihanna or anyone else, had been on my radar for a while (especially when my kids were in the car with me, which was 99.9% of the time), but it was not until that hot, summer day that I connected the dots. *Even if she didn't understand what she was singing, the message was still being taken into her impressionable brain and internalized in her heart.* It was that moment I switched from the popular hits station to Christian music just. like. that. I'd never listened to Christian music before that day. I'd seen a billboard with the call letters and turned the dial. I mean, if my kids were going to internalize a message about anything, I'd rather it be about God than the smell of sex in the air, for Pete's sake!

The car ride ended up being the tip of the iceberg of my awareness and the changes I slowly but steadily made in my life. Waking up to what I was ingesting through the media, in my marriage and friendships, and through my relationship with each of my kids consciously shifted to become a practice of curious self-inquiry that continues today.

My daughter, as well as my sons (at the time 6, 11, and 16), were just as happy listening to Christian music. I don't remember any of them giving me crap about missing the top hits station or any eye rolls around the genre of our new music choice. In fact, for years now when Maddux goes to bed at night, he tunes in to the same local Christian station on his clock radio and it plays all night long while he sleeps (though during the day I will tell you he'd listen to anything but Christian or country music).

Did I get zero pushback about the switch in stations because my kids never gave me a hard time or because they were extraordinarily easy-going human beings? Absolutely not! They didn't resist because they understood that this was a change we were making, from the tone of my voice, my behavior, and the energy I was putting out.

I was clear.

That's what it means to be an intentional parent. The clarity in your mind and body about your boundaries and paying attention to your emotional well-being allows you to be attuned to your family's emotions and, with continued awareness and practice, consistent in your parenting. *Our children need for us to be clear, intentional, and conscious in our lives, so we can be emotionally attuned to them as we support and guide them into who they're meant to be.*

They say you can never be fully prepared to parent; I believe this is the truth. We could, however, better know our authentic selves and have clarity around who we believe we are. Instead, in order to please our parents, before we even know we are doing it, we take on beliefs and identities that simply aren't true in order to gain love and acceptance. In the same unconscious state, we then project the pattern onto our kids. It is time for this to stop.

Come with me as I explore the limiting beliefs I unconsciously took on during my childhood, the ones I lived out over and over again in adulthood until recently when I put them under a microscope. Taking the time to uncover my beliefs and ask the essential question, "Is this true?" has been the foundation of my awakening. My intention through sharing my story in the pages ahead is to inspire you to examine your own beliefs, question them, and then shift those that don't resonate with who you truly are. I want for you to choose to become the person you are meant to be and the parent your child needs you to be!

And now, let's begin the process of looking back to move forward.

Becoming Me

THE MYTHS I TOOK ON ABOUT MYSELF

I AM NOT WORTHY OF BEING HEARD

One of my favorite things to do as a little girl was to swing on the swings. We had one of those classic swing sets with the flimsy plastic seats and metal poles in our backyard, but my best friend Mary, who lived next door, had a playground-quality poles-cemented-in-the-ground swing set with wood seats and I could go over there anytime, even if they weren't home. One Wisconsin summer night when I was six years old, that's what my four-year-old and two-year-old brothers and I did. My dad was outside talking to my aunt who was over dropping something off as the boys and I walked across the driveway to my neighbor's swing set. We were easily seen by the adults because we had small backyards and open fences.

Mary also had a big sandbox. She was the youngest of four kids and her three older brothers were no longer interested in the backyard play equipment, so Mary pretty much had it all to herself. Her family was up north on vacation at the time, so the boys and I had the whole yard to ourselves.

My youngest brother, Rob, toddled over to the sandbox to play as Paul and I headed to the swings. Talking and laughing, we were enjoying our last shot at outdoor play on this summer evening before it got dark and we had to head inside to bed. I suggested we have a contest to see who could swing the highest, and Paul agreed.

Game on! We both worked hard at pumping our little legs to gain momentum. We were both going strong when Rob decided he wanted to swing, too. He was making his way towards us and babbling something, but my desire to beat my brother and my laughter didn't allow me to hear him. He crept closer to my swing. I turned my head to see he was getting closer and yelled, "Stop!"

I yelled at him again. I didn't want to hit him as he was almost in front of me. I knew I needed to stop myself quickly and knew how to drag my feet to do that, but everything happened too fast for me to be able to stop in time—and BAM! I collided with my little brother, knocking him over. He fell to the ground under my swing, and I hit him again as the swing came back down! My stomach dropped. I hit him not once, but twice, before I gained control of my swing. I'll never forget that sound of the thud as I hit his little body and the way it felt as the impact vibrated through the swing.

His screams brought my dad and my aunt racing across the driveway and into the neighbor's yard. By then, I'd bent down and tried to hug my brother who was screaming and crying. I was crying, too, because I knew he was hurt and it was my fault. I loved my baby brother, and I would never want to intentionally hurt him.

I stood back. Paul had abandoned his swing at this point, too. We both knew that, in an instant, the fun summer night had taken a complete turn.

My dad scooped Rob up in his arms and he and my aunt looked over my brother. My mom was out for the evening, so dad was in charge. My dad looked up at me and yelled, "Go to your room, now!"

I tried to explain what had happened, but my brother's crying and my dad's expression told me I'd better shut up and move.

Climbing the stairs to my room, I wiped more tears off my cheeks. How badly was Rob hurt? Did I do permanent damage? I felt sick. I laid down on my bed and continued to cry, filled with a mixture of sadness and anger.

A few minutes later I heard my mom pull into the garage, followed by my parents' voices downstairs as she and my dad talked. At that point, Rob had calmed down somewhat. Mom took him while dad came upstairs. He got Paul ready for bed before coming to see me.

Dad entered my room. Once again, I tried to tell him what had happened. I could see from his expression he was still very angry. He cut me off and told me I should have been more careful and aware of what my brother was doing; it was my fault he was hurt. Then he came over and spanked me. This was an unusual response in our home but one that made an undeniable and lasting impression.

That summer evening, I learned what I had to say didn't matter.

I NEED TO PERFORM FOR LOVE AND APPROVAL

On a dark, cold winter night, wind whipped through the bare branches of the large oak tree outside my bedroom window as I lay curled up on my side in bed, quietly crying, waiting for my mom to come tuck me in and say good night. Though I didn't want her to feel my tears when she bent over to kiss my cheek, I knew I wouldn't be able to keep my voice from quivering when she asked me if everything was okay. It wasn't. My mom, my rock, was leaving early the next morning. Even at the tender age of eight, I understood she deserved a break from my brothers and me and all parents occasionally needed to take vacations; still, I wanted to beg her to stay home. And, of course, that's exactly what I did.

I could tell by the sound of her voice it hurt my mom's heart to be firm with me, telling me she knew I could be a big girl. She told me how much my grandparents would appreciate me being strong and helping with my little brothers, and in no time at all the week would go by and she'd be back home. She acknowledged my articulated fear—yes, sometimes planes did crash—but she was sure God would bring her back home safely to us and she would be so excited to see me then.

There was no swaying her. She kissed me on the forehead one more time, told me to be a good girl at school, and promised she would call to check in a few days later. I watched her silhouette move away from me as she walked out of my room. More tears streamed from my eyes. I sniffled, wiping the snot running from my nose on the top sheet. I desperately wanted to be the strong girl she told me I could be, the one she wanted me to be for her.

But the truth is that when my mom wasn't nearby, I was a wreck. I didn't feel comfortable or confident. When she wasn't with me — whether she was nearby at the grocery store, or, in this case, going to California on vacation with my dad for a week — I was scared she wouldn't come back.

When I revisit this period of anxiety with my mom, she believes the start of my anxiety came from an incident in first grade when a boy in my class, Tim Higgins, lost his mom to cancer. Then, when I was in second grade, my good friend Mary Ann Horkheimer's mom had a stillborn baby. I went to a Catholic school, which meant we attended the funerals; I remember seeing the big casket (it was my very first funeral) and then, a year later, seeing the tiny casket. My young mind made the connection that if other people's moms and babies can die, then so could my mom. I wondered how I could possibly continue to exist if I lost my mom? According to my mom, it was the later part of second grade when my anxiety appeared.

My parents' vacation to Palm Springs is the earliest recollection I have of experiencing the separation anxiety that lasted several years. At times, it was hard to function; it disrupted an otherwise happy childhood, and, occasionally, my parents lost their patience with me: my dad more quickly than my mom. Many playdates and sleepovers were ruined or cut short by my sudden stomach aches. It would happen when I was playing with my best friend next door, or with my cousin and her family (she and I are a year apart and loved spending time with one another during our childhood). Things got really out of hand in fourth grade when my parents moved us mid-year and I had to start at a new school.

Their decision to move began on a Sunday drive out to the country in the fall of 1976 when they found their dream home on a lake about 30 miles outside of town. We moved over Christmas break and I left the only home I'd ever known, my best friend, and the familiarity of everything. There wasn't enough room for my brothers and I to go to the Catholic school in our new town to finish out the school year together. So I went to the local public school until the fall when the Catholic school hopefully would have room for all three of us. This meant starting a new school twice during the year ahead.

If my anxiety was bad before the move, it definitely ramped up once I entered public school. There were so many kids! The new school I started after Christmas was only K-5 but, even though my old school spanned grades 1-8, it felt bigger, noisier, and super intimidating to a quiet, shy girl like me. I'm not sure where I picked up that I was shy — maybe I heard my mom tell someone that in passing — but I wore the label like a name badge.

I did not feel comfortable introducing myself or trying to talk with kids I didn't know. My fourth-grade teacher was very nice and I'm sure she tried to get me involved by introducing me to a few really nice girls who might take me in, but the only person who sticks out from that six-month stint is Tina Hutchison. For some reason, what I remember most about Tina is that she lived with her grandparents, which I thought was strange. One Saturday, my mom dropped me off at Tina's for a playdate. While I don't recall what we did, I do remember being relieved when my mom showed up in the driveway a few hours later to take me home.

The epitome of how my anxiety drove me brings me to the story of my running away. For weeks, I'd been faking stomach aches at school, and my mom had picked me up from the nurse's office at least ten times. At first she was sympathetic. But by this point she was getting really angry at me because it would interrupt her day for her to drive 15 minutes each way, and once she got me home I'd be fine. Mom could not figure me out and, though I am sure she was worried about me, she was about done with my shenanigans.

I couldn't stop worrying about my mom and wanting to be with her when I was at school. I was barely tolerating the second half of fourth grade, though previously I'd been a good student. So, one day in April 1977, while sitting in language arts, I had a brilliant idea. I decided I would run away from school during recess. I can still remember sitting in the back of the room at my desk, trying hard to stay focused on the worksheet in front of me as the plan began forming in my head. It was springtime and still cold out, so I briefly worried about whether or not the windbreaker I wore to school that day would be warm enough for the long walk. My trips to the nurse's office were getting so frequent my teacher finally got smart and had a student escort me to and from the bathroom if I asked to go. Jesus! But they left me alone on the playground. And Tina was gone for the day, which meant I had no one to talk to; I just wanted to get the hell out of there.

I barely ate lunch because I was so excited! (Who am I kidding? I barely ate lunch any day. I kept thinking I was going to throw up, so I never ate much at all while at school.) My plan was to sneak through the woods and then connect with my bus route and walk that route back home. I didn't think it would take me that long to walk, maybe an hour or two, which didn't worry me at all. Again, I was not thinking beyond this brilliant idea I'd come up with to get out of half the school day.

The bell finally rang and we were dismissed by grade level. Out on the playground I zipped up my blue windbreaker. Maybe it would be a little colder than I thought—even in April, Wisconsin was chilly. Still, I was determined.

I watched the playground duty teachers hover near the corner of the building, chatting among themselves as I slowly crept toward the woods. The further I got from the building, the more confident I became. When I thought it was safe, I turned and ran towards the woods, thinking, "They're not gonna stop me now!"

A few minutes later, I had made my way through the woods and onto the road that passed through the small downtown area and led to my bus route.

Traveling on foot provided a different view than peering from the bus windows. As I walked along the road through town, there were a lot of cars whizzing by. I briefly wondered if anyone would stop and ask me what I was doing. If they did, what would I say? After all, I was clearly a kid who was supposed to be in school. But no one stopped, and I made the first turn out of the busy town onto the first long, winding, narrow road. The few vehicles I saw whizzed along, unconcerned by my midday walk along the road. I remember passing by a dead-end road where the bus turned to pick up another fourth grader named Debbie and her younger brother.

The walk was taking much longer than I thought. I left the playground about 11:45 a.m. In my nine-year-old mind I thought I'd walk in the front door with a smile on my face (as if my mom would be glad to see me) by about 1:00 p.m. Why did I think my mom would somehow accept the fact that I'd walked home from school in the middle of the day? I have no idea because that's definitely not what happened.

Finally, after what felt like forever, I turned into our cul-de-sac. I walked to our front door and rang the bell. No answer. Weird. I looked into the garage window and saw Mom's car was gone. Where could she be? I was standing on the driveway trying to figure out how to get in the house when our neighbor, Mrs. Brown, yelled, "Kim! Kim, where have you been?! Your mother is worried sick and she's out looking for you." Mrs. Brown waved at me to come over, so I did. I liked Mrs. Brown; she had six kids, one of whom was my only other friend, her youngest daughter Debbie. Mrs. Brown was a nice lady, in my experience. The Brown kids went to a different school than I did. It would have been a lot easier if we'd gone to the same school and rode the same bus. Debbie and I often played near the lake after school and on weekends. We liked to play house in the trees and use the seaweed that washed up on the beach as "food" to serve our pretend families. Mrs. Brown brought me into their house. I could tell she was a little frantic as she called my school to tell them I was okay. Mrs. Brown put me in front of some cartoons while we waited for my mom to come. Without cell phones, I have no idea whether they relayed the message to my mom or if, at some point, my mom just decided to come home, hoping to God I was there. Sitting in front of Mrs. Brown's television was the first moment I actually thought about how the school might react to my leaving, what a call like that might do to my mom, and how much trouble I might be in for going through with my "brilliant" idea. (This was not the last of my brilliant ideas in life but it illustrates how children often can't, and don't, grasp the consequences of their actions).

Soon my mom showed up at the Browns' door. Her expression seemed to be a mixture of relief, anger, fear, and I-don't-know-what-to-do-with-you-anymore. She hugged me and we walked home. On the way to our house, Mom told me I needed to go to my room. I think she probably needed some time to come down off the adrenaline of knowing I'd chosen to walk off the playground and spent several hours walking on twisty, narrow country roads. (I imagine she said things like: "Do you know you could have been hit and killed?" "Do you know someone could have come along and abducted you and we'd never see you again?" "Do you have any idea how dangerous what you did was????")

I don't know if my mom called my dad at work before he came home to tell him what happened or if she unloaded when he walked in the door, but a few minutes after he got home my bedroom door opened and there he stood, wielding my mom's hairbrush. I was lying on my stomach on my bed trying to read a book and my first instinct was to turn over and sit up to protect my butt. He was angry; his expression said it all. I didn't see any indication on his face that said, "I was worried about you and what could have happened to you." He asked me to turn over and then he said, "This is gonna hurt me a lot more than it's gonna hurt you." And he beat me with the hairbrush.

It was painful; each swat stung more than the last as I

instinctively clenched my butt cheeks. I couldn't recover before the next one came. My dad was taking out his anger, frustration, and lack of parenting skill on my bottom, but the damage was much more than skin deep. His fear, frustration, lack of knowledge, and disconnection from his own feelings directly affected my core as a human being worthy of empathy, understanding, and connection. To be clear, physical discipline didn't happen often in our house, but this wasn't the first time he'd taken out his disappointment in me on my rear end.

That moment created an indelible mark on my soul and created my belief that I needed to behave the way my parents wanted me to in order to feel loved. In my mind, my relationship with my dad was never quite the same after the hairbrush incident.

My mom and dad said they loved my brothers and me unconditionally but the tone of their voices, the expectations they set — spoken and unspoken — and the energy they projected gave me a very clear sense of whether what they said and what they believed were in sync. My parents couldn't help it; it was the way they were raised, as well. For generations, we've been telling kids we love them unconditionally, yet as parents, we make the conditions through which they gain that love clear.

It was close to the end of the school year on the day I ran away. Since the school year was nearly over when I ran away, my parents agreed that Mom would pick me up for lunch and recess every day so I could get through the day.

Even though I got to skip lunch and recess at school, their plan was still really tough on me. I continued to put my mom through the ringer by crying each time she drove me back to school after lunch. It seemed like every time she drove me back to school the song "Dust in the Wind" by Kansas played on the radio. God, that song makes me feel sick. Even now, on rare occasions when I hear it on the radio, I have to turn it off. I still have a physical reaction to the song.

That summer, I was fine, a normal nine-year-old turning ten years old. In the fall, I started the Catholic school that finally had room for me, along with my brothers. My anxiety had all but vanished over the summer while I was home with my family and I'd love to tell you it didn't resurface with the start of the school year but, of course, it resurfaced. I found myself in the nurse's office on the very first morning. Somehow, though, probably through lots of my mom's prayers and divine intervention, I managed to make a good friend pretty quickly. While I still had stomach issues, I eventually settled into fifth grade, and never contemplated running away from the playground during recess. Of course, the Catholic school was twice as far from home as my previous school so I think I'd learned my lesson the first time around.

Things were relatively calm and I did okay in school, even participating in cheerleading while attending St. Bruno's in

Dousman, WI. I was just getting comfortable when, once again, my parents decided to move.

Through these childhood experiences, my beliefs were being reinforced that I wasn't worthy of being heard and that, in order to earn my parents' love and acceptance, I needed to be a good girl and do as I was told.

I CAN'T TRUST MYSELF

The dream house on the lake in the country was too much work and too far away from my dad's job to enjoy the way my parents had anticipated, so the summer before I entered junior high, we moved back into town. We didn't return to the same city, mind you. Returning to the first school I'd enjoyed would have been a welcome step. Instead, we moved to a different town in the suburbs and, once again, a new Catholic school.

Though the anxiety about being away from mom gradually dissipated, it was replaced by a preoccupation with the opposite sex. Around the time we moved, boys began to land on my radar as something more than just loud, obnoxious, disruptive people in the classroom. It also felt like a way to get some attention and the topic of dating began to infiltrate all the conversations I had with my new friends. We wondered to one another, "Do you think he's cute? Do you think he likes me?" Fortunately, with boys to bond us, making friends this time around wasn't as hard as it had been in the last move. I'm sure that was a relief to my parents—the friend part, not the boy part.

My first experience with a boyfriend occurred only a few months into seventh grade. At first, it started with lingering looks and shy smiles as we passed one another in the hallways while changing classes, then it progressed to note passing (often his friends gave it to one of mine and, three people later, I'd get the note). I'm sure those notes said intriguing things such as, "I like Queen's new album, do you?" Still, as a 12-year-old girl, it was enough to make my heart skip a beat.

People warned me he was a "user" and not to get involved with him (he apparently already had a reputation). Being innocently unaware of his ulterior motives, his attention, which I strongly desired, was too tempting to turn down. It wasn't long before his notes progressed to invitations to meet in the woods near our house. And naïve as I was, I agreed. It felt so good to be noticed.

My friends were right. He was a user, a "wise man" of thirteen who shared a few well-chosen compliments to get what he really wanted. This was my first real experience of trading my sense of self to be accepted by someone other than my parents and friends.

I cultivated the habit of figuring out how to be who others needed or wanted me to be in order to feel worthy of their acceptance, affection, appreciation, attention, and connection. So, my first "relationship" lasted a hot minute and led, in part, to a series of additional short, meaningless-note-passing, meet-me-in-the-woods relationships that peppered my junior high years.

Not coincidentally, some of my friends were going down the

same path and we counseled one another through our heartaches. Needless to say, with all the amateur romance and drama, my grades were the last thing to which I paid attention. And yet, the lower my grades ranked in my life, the more important they seemed to become to my parents, especially my dad.

In the spring of my eighth-grade year, I had an experience that solidified my belief that my body was my best avenue for attention from boys. One Saturday evening, I was babysitting for my parent's friends, who had four kids. The two boys were close in age to me, which made it difficult to get them to listen to me or to go to bed when it was time. This particular night, my parents were actually out with the parents of the kids I was babysitting.

Of course, my friends knew where I was babysitting and I'm sure I let a few of the boys know as well. Early in the night, Mark, a boy from the other eighth grade class (who I thought was super cute), called the house and I answered. He told me he had a few friends sleeping over and they were looking for something to do; he asked if I wanted visitors. "I have to get the kids to bed, so give me until 10:30," I told him I'd babysat for these people before and knew they never came home early, so I didn't expect them to come home until midnight. I also knew it was wrong to have them over but I was thirteen and trying to become popular.

I managed to get the kids settled down and shortly after, as I was watching television in the family room, I heard laughter and tapping at the window. The boys had arrived. Mark was there with three boys from my Catholic school and my best friend Lisa's older brother John, who was in high school. I opened the back door and we talked and laughed through the screen door for about ten minutes. Then Mark suggested I come outside so we could all play hacky sack on the patio.

Without hesitating, I agreed. These were boys I went to school with every day and I knew John pretty well, too, since I spent a lot of time at Lisa's house. I grabbed my jacket and went out to the patio. We started to play hacky sack. Admittedly, I was not very good at it since I felt this was a boy's game and I'd played only once or twice.

After a few minutes of kicking the small bean bag between us on the patio, the boys just kind of stopped and, for some reason, I got this weird feeling (that I now recognize as intuition) up my back. Then, totally unexpectedly, they all began taking steps toward me. We weren't more than a few yards away from one another on the patio. My instinct said "Run!" so I turned away from them and took off, running out into the backyard. The motion detector went off and a good portion of the backyard was illuminated. I could hear them right behind me. Not knowing what to do but very quickly understanding things had shifted from their being friendly to my needing to be on the defense, I continued to run. We lived in an area with 1+ acre lots but it wasn't long before they caught me and tackled me to the ground. All I could think was,

"Jesus, I hope the kids are asleep and not watching out the window." The girls' bedroom was in the front of the house, but the boys' rooms overlooked the backyard. Looking back, it seems odd that I didn't yell for them to help, but I think I just didn't want them to see what happened.

It's hard to write about an experience you'd rather forget, and this is one of those. It's embarrassing to remember and share; in hindsight, it's hard not to feel like I should have known what was coming and why the boys wanted to visit that night. I feel ashamed, like it was somehow my fault it happened. My sense of trust in human beings was totally shaken. Once again, like the beating my dad had given me in my most vulnerable moment, my innocence was literally pulled out from under me.

Four boys on one girl—not fair. I knew I wasn't capable of fighting to get away as they held down parts of my body, one at each of my arms and one for my legs while the other took joy in my pubescent body. My clothes were pulled up, down, and shifted; my writhing was nothing against their strength and I will never forget the taste and smell of their hands over my mouth.

After what seemed like an eternity, but was probably only a few minutes, they got up and ran away as I sat up in a daze, wondering what the fuck had happened. I was stunned, shocked, but knew I had to get my shit together, get back in the house, and keep it together until the parents returned.

So that's what I did: I sat up and I righted my clothing, standing up while shifting and righting some more. Then I walked back into the house, telling myself what a fucking idiot I was for coming outside. For literally playing right into their hands. For not seeing anything out of the ordinary was possible. I went to school, to church, with these boys every week! My best friend's older brother, for God's sake! Two thoughts continued to simultaneously go through my mind: *How could they do this to me?!* And *how could I be such a dumb ass??*

I went to the bathroom and splashed cold water on my face and then returned to watching television just like I had been before they showed up. A few minutes later, I heard the garage door open and the car pull in the garage. When the parents came in, I smiled, said the kids were all great that night. They paid me and the dad drove me five minutes home. I walked in the front door and up the stairs, said goodnight to my mom, and got ready for bed. I crawled into my bed and started bawling.

I'm so glad I did what I did next. I went down the hall and asked my mom to come to my room so I could talk to her. I'm sure she was shocked at my face. She quickly followed me down the hall; I sat on my bed and poured out to her exactly what had happened. Thank God, she didn't get mad at me for any of it, she said she was so sorry that I'd gone through that ordeal. She asked me to share it the next day with the woman I babysat for (also my mom's friend) because she thought it was important her friend knew in case one of her kids had actually seen anything.

The next morning the woman came over and we sat at our kitchen table while I told her the story. Through tears, I apologized for having visitors over while I was babysitting her kids, acknowledging it was wrong to have done that. Fortunately, she was as empathetic as my mom was, which was, again, very helpful and needed at the time. She appreciated my honesty; none of the kids had mentioned hearing or seeing anything but she was glad she knew in case it came up later.

My mom also told my dad and he called each of the boys and told them to come over immediately. They must have decided it would be better to come as a group because they all showed up on their bikes at the same time. It was warm enough I had my bedroom windows open so I heard my dad go out the front door and meet them in our driveway. His voice was filled with anger and, though I couldn't hear everything he was saying to them, I did hear him call them a bunch of filthy pigs, which made me happy, though they deserved much more.

And that was it. My dad never brought up the subject to me, my parents never said anything more about it and life went on. I still had to go to school the next day, though, and sit in the same classes with three of those boys until we graduated eighth grade a few weeks later. I don't remember even telling my friend Lisa, I did however avoid going over to her house for some time.

Every once in a while, one of them would make a comment I could clearly overhear in the hallways. It was nerve-racking. While I generally tried not to look at any of them, I happened to do so while in church during our graduation practice and two of them were sitting next to one another; they basically looked at me like they'd gotten away with murder.

Looking back on the situation, I realize my parents should have called the police. It was clearly sexual assault. Maybe they contemplated it, but thought that might make things worse for me so they didn't. Maybe, because these boys were well-known in our neighborhood, they didn't want to deal with their parents. My best friend's father was a prominent lawyer; perhaps that scared my dad. I don't know their reasoning but, for years, I wondered if they didn't call the police because, on some level, they thought it was my fault the abuse happened. At this point, I tell myself they didn't get the police involved because they just didn't know what to do. As an adult and a parent, having lived the experience, I can say for certain the boys sexually assaulted me against my will.

This is when I learned I couldn't trust others, even those I thought I knew well, and even more than that, I could not trust myself.

I'LL NEVER BE GOOD ENOUGH

As I continued through my teen years, friendships and romantic relationships with boys became increasingly important. Ironically, even though by my freshman year in high school boys were the center of my life, I chose to go to an all-girls, Catholic high school. To be honest, I wasn't all that jazzed about the idea but it was where most of my good friends were going and, since my brief, unhappy stint in public school during the second half of fourth grade, I really had no desire to go to the public high school. Even knowing I would see and interact with boys every day wasn't enough incentive.

The Catholic prep school I attended drew from the entire Milwaukee metroplex and had an all-boys counterpart campus across town. All of our school's social activities were scheduled around the boys' football games and each school's monthly mixers. It was a well-known fact you wanted to date a guy from that school. So, of course, staying in touch with boys from my grade school who ended up going to the all-boys high school was a great way to get to know some of the other boys.

One of my neighbors became my fixation from sophomore year until I was a senior, mainly because he went to the right school and occasionally paid attention to me. Though I dated a few other guys during high school, he was my first "true love," among other things. We dated on and off, which really meant he called me and found a way for us to spend time together when he wanted to screw around; otherwise, he really didn't care to talk to me. To me, our relationship was very meaningful. To him, I think I was just a warm body who gave him the time of day. I cringe when I think about how little I thought of myself and how desperately I was looking for male attention.

At one point during my junior year, I dated a football player who wanted me to have sex and I told him I couldn't because I was saving myself for someone else. The relationship ended shortly thereafter. The lesson I learned there was I really had just one choice: to put out or become history. My friends were all finding the same to be true with their boyfriends. We were all gaga over these stupid boys from the private boys' school and literally let them have their way with us because it was so important to be dating one of them. They could probably smell the opportunity from a mile away.

High school was not a favorite chapter in my life. I was not a great student; it wasn't that I was dumb, but I had more important things to worry about than getting good grades. Maybe I was afraid to apply myself because I just didn't have much faith in my ability. Maybe I graduated with a 2.3 GPA because my parents were so adamant about grades and, subconsciously, I rebelled. Maybe I just didn't give a shit, I don't know. I had a handful of good friends and we all worked at being accepted by the popular girls. Our families had money, but many of our peers came from a lot more and everyone knew the kids with money were the popular kids around whom everyone wanted to hang. Overall, I worked just hard enough to get by. In the mid-1980s it wasn't hard to get accepted into a state university, so when it came time to apply, I went along with the crowd and chose to go to the school four hours from home where most of my friends also applied.

Another activity I was involved in during my junior/senior years was going to the dive bars in downtown Milwaukee roughly a 30-minute drive from home. A couple of college campus bars would let us in, no questions asked. Many school nights, I told my mom I had to go to the library to study and would instead go downtown with friends for an hour at the bar, then return home without any questions asked. This clearly could not have helped my grade point average, but what the hell, we were teenagers out for a good time! Consequences? What consequences? (Please tell me I'm not the only one who didn't think about what might happen if I made a stupid choice?)

My parents began to suspect my drinking. The difficulty I had getting out of bed some mornings, and my mood swings when it came to boys were contributing factors. If all was well in my world, I'd be in a great mood: happy and cheerful. If things weren't going well (boy said he'd call but didn't, boy didn't ask me out, etc.), I was definitely down and had to drag myself out of bed. In the late spring of my junior year, I was driven home one night after puking all over and then my dad had to literally carry me into the house. My mom was worried enough about me that she searched my room, found my diary under my bed and cut through the cheap lock. I am sure you can imagine how graphic a teenage girl might be about everything, from experiences with boys to family issues and situations involving school and teachers. She read it all. Then she showed my dad.

The worst part about the entire ordeal — beyond the fact I was ashamed, livid, and completely humiliated by what they'd both read — was that, when I got home from school and they confronted me with this horror, my Dad called me a slut. That four-letter word coming from his mouth slammed into me with greater force than the beating with a hairbrush. You don't forget when your dad calls you a slut. The reality was I was looking for acceptance and attention in the wrong places and, now, the person whose admiration I most wanted had pierced my heart.

My mom was less concerned about the intimate details in the book and more concerned by the fact she had no idea I'd been going out to bars. She didn't tell me she was hurt, that I'd broken the trust we had, but I felt it. My dad didn't know how to deal with any of it other than to show his anger by being condescending and spitting hurtful names at me, perhaps in a failed attempt to disguise his love and concern.

I spent the rest of the school year and the summer grounded

from my friends. Of course, this didn't stop me. Though I wasn't consciously trying to piss off my parents, I was seventeen and more concerned with having a good time. I just learned I had to be sneakier in my fun.

Coincidentally, and fortunately, a guy I'd gone to grade school with began showing interest in me. He was now on the football team at the boys' school and he was in GREAT shape. He was a very nice boy and my parents really liked and trusted him, so they let me date him when the opportunity arrived. THAT was my ticket out of the house!

We didn't date for long, just enough to get me through the summer and back in my parent's reasonably good graces before I cut it off. I truly don't think he was all that heartbroken; I think the feeling was mutual. Looking back on it now, he truly was (and is) a genuinely nice guy, and gentleman, and I still feel guilty for using him that summer. (I'm so sorry, John!)

Once senior year began, it was back to the bars for me! With additional precautions, I got through my final year of high school without much incident. The night before my high school graduation I was bar-hopping downtown, yet again, and had a few too many brandy-and-cokes before heading to the parking lot with Rob, a guy who had been a friend for about a year. My close friend, Kathy, had been dating his friend for months, so we'd spent a fair amount of casual time together—and I'd thought he was cute for quite a while. The liquid courage I had consumed over the previous hours made me bold enough to let him know how I felt and, unsurprisingly, we ended up making out. It was the beginning of the first really serious dating relationship I had where I felt I actually meant something to someone. His attention and praise were just what I craved.

Each of these experiences made me believe I'd never be good enough in my parents' eyes, or be cute enough to hold onto a relationship with a boy. Love was conditional, and using my body to get attention was a useful, yet self-deprecating, way to feed my desire for both.

After that night in the parking lot of the bar, Rob and I were hot and heavy from then on. He showed up at my graduation ceremony the next night and we spent every possible moment we could together that summer before I left for college. Rob was a year older than me. He was taking some classes at a local university, but wasn't a very serious student. His father had died the previous year of pancreatic cancer and he'd left each of his kids some money, so working was not Rob's priority. Spending time tinkering with his black 1978 Camaro with the Hurst T-shift was his greatest joy. Spending time and money on me was a close second. It. was. amazing!

Based on Dad's vibe and comments, I pretty much knew he disliked Rob from the beginning. Dad wanted me to work and save money for school but, as a teen in love, I found every excuse I could to spend time with Rob. There were a tense few months at home because, while I'd occasionally missed my curfew before, when Rob and I began dating it was a true indication of my wanting to be out of my parents' house, making my own rules. I'm sure my parents felt somewhat relieved when August rolled around and it was time to move me into the dorm. Knowing Rob was staying in town and taking classes on another campus four hours away, they thought (and likely prayed) we'd eventually break up. They were wrong.

While I did party with my roommate, who I knew fairly well from high school, I saw Rob every weekend from the beginning of the semester until Christmas. Sometimes he drove up to campus and spent the weekend; other times, I got a ride or took a Greyhound bus back to Milwaukee, and spent the weekend in a hotel or (on occasion) went home.

Spending the weekend at home meant I actually had less time with Rob, both because my parents actually wanted to spend time with me and because I had a curfew. If I stayed in a hotel, Rob and I had every moment together from the time I arrived until the time I left. Since he was nineteen, Rob's mom pretty much let him do what he wanted. Besides, she may have been side-tracked with grief from her husband's death. She didn't parent much, not like my parents did, anyway. But then, I was the oldest of three children while Rob was the baby of his family. He had three older brothers living at home and his oldest sibling, the only sister, was married, had a daughter, and lived ninety miles away in Madison.

One weekend that fall, I got caught sneaking back to Milwaukee by my parents, even though the hotel where I stayed was way across town from our house. My mom called the dorm and my roommate answered the phone in our room. She inadvertently told Mom I wasn't in La Crosse. My roommate called me immediately, feeling awful she'd made the mistake, and told me my mom wanted me to call her right away. Knowing I was busted, I called Mom but refused to come home. I told her I was safe, not to worry about me, and I was heading back to campus the next day. During my first semester of college, I was in Milwaukee more than I was in LaCrosse—and I sure as hell wasn't concentrating on my school work. That's the kind of crazy thing young love will do to a girl.

When I came home from college for Christmas break, I was met by some pretty cranky parents. My grades weren't great (as usual). They knew by then I was not only having sex but also sneaking around while they were basically throwing money away on an education I wasn't taking advantage of having. My dad, in particular, made it clear he was disappointed in me, again.

My brothers were attending the all-boys school, following in my dad's footsteps as he also had attended there. Dad worried about the kind of example I was setting for them with my lack of motivation to earn a college degree. Most of the conversations my dad and I had in my teen years, particularly during that semester, revolved around his lectures on how shitty my grades were and how I wouldn't go anywhere in life if I kept shutting doors on myself. I was not concerned. I was eighteen years old, in love, and thought I had the world by the balls.

I was smart enough to go to Planned Parenthood when I arrived on campus in the fall. Somehow, I escaped pregnancy the first few months Rob and I dated that summer, but I knew I needed to get on the pill as soon as possible. However, that protection didn't last long. When I came home for Thanksgiving, in my rush to pack, I forgot my pills. My roommate was staying on campus an extra day and I called her, freaking out, asking her to bring them to me the next day but, by the time I actually had them in hand, it was Saturday and I had missed two pills. I knew it wasn't possible to take that many at once and I'd need to have a period before I started the next pack. Like the naïve teenager I was, I told myself I'd be protected over Thanksgiving break because I'd been faithfully taking them until I had left campus Thursday. It's amazing what you can talk yourself into, you know?

To add drama to the story, the week before Thanksgiving, I woke up in the middle of the night with absolutely horrendous pain in my lower back. I tried to quietly get up and use the shared bathroom down the hall. Amidst the pain, I found I could not pee and really felt horrible, so I went back to our room, woke up my roommate, and she got the Resident Assistant. The three of us took a cab to the local hospital where I stayed two nights trying to deliver a kidney stone. It was the most physically painful situation I had ever experienced.

At the hospital, they put me on several medications, including antibiotics. They didn't tell me some of those medications can compromise the effectiveness of birth control pills. I learned that later — at my first prenatal visit.

So, I went into Thanksgiving weekend unaware that my birth control coverage was compromised by the medication. Then I forgot to pack the pills and didn't get them in time to continue the monthly regimen. But knowing this did not stop me from having sex with Rob that weekend.

Discovering I was pregnant, and then having to tell my parents, was mostly frightening, but also a little exciting. News like that is hard to wrap your head around at first. This wonderfully fun act resulted in a human being! That's some crazy shit, right?

It didn't take long to feel like an alien among my college freshman friends. They were worrying about what to wear to the next party while I weighed my options. My mind reeled with questions. Should I stay pregnant? Who was I kidding? How could I possibly be a mom at eighteen? Should I give my baby up for adoption instead? How will my life turn out? Would I even be a good mom? Motherhood is like a really long babysitting job where you never get a break or get to go home without the kid. I enjoyed babysitting, but motherhood was an entirely different prospect.

Ack! The emotions I experienced added to the drama with both Rob and my parents during the next eight months was exhausting. My gut kept telling me it would all work out fine; I would be a great mom and the rest would fall into place, somehow. But Rob did not believe the same and he wasn't ready to be a dad. My parents (mainly my dad) did not see any future for me if I kept the baby and gave up on the dismal college education I was halfheartedly trying to pursue.

But you know what? My life felt purposeful for the first time ever. I was only going to college because it was the "right" next step after high school. I had no idea what I wanted to be at the age of 18 (other than someone who enjoyed a good party and appreciated cute boys who paid attention to me).

When I was pregnant and having to make really big decisions about who I was and how I was handling my life, I felt like the baby inside me gave me purpose. Plus, aside from some occasional nausea, and a total aversion to mayonnaise, I really enjoyed being pregnant. Except for the weight gain. As I neared the end of nine months, I gained 60 pounds (putting my 5'3" frame at 150 pounds). It was summer and most of my friends were walking around in tank tops and bikinis. And while it may not have been so cool, I loved the feeling of the baby moving around inside me and I couldn't wait to hold him!

As my pregnancy progressed, I was excited about becoming a mom while Rob was really just going along for the ride because he felt he loved me. On some level, as much as he was able to love me, he did. But as time went on and our relationship got more stressful as the responsibilities grew more layered, it became more about him wanting to control and manipulate me than about actual love. Rob had a terrible temper; he was reckless and thoughtless when driving angry. He was emotionally immature and it came out in anger, frustration, and threats. There were several nights we would go out, and he'd end up drunk and full of rage. He'd then drive his Camaro way over the speed limit while I sat in the passenger seat, tightly gripping the door and praying to God I'd be able to get home in one piece, still pregnant. Just before my due date, I finally found the courage to advocate for myself and told Rob I really needed the safety, security, and support of my mom during labor and delivery. He just wasn't gonna cut it. I felt he was relieved but would not ever say that he was. He showed up–because it looked good–to hold my hand until things got really bad and it was time to be wheeled into delivery. Then he called his friend and they met in the parking lot to smoke weed while I delivered our son, Nick. This was typical nineteen-year-old behavior, but in my mind, I continued the delusion he was capable of much more.

It was easy to see that in order to be seen, feel loved, and be secure I gravitated to making unhealthy choices.

BE CAREFUL WITH MONEY

My first experience with birth was probably as physically painful as having a kidney stone, only birth was quicker. The kidney stone took forty-eight hours to pass and, once I passed it, I felt completely fine. On the other hand, though giving birth came after about nine hours of labor, recovering from being stitched up took weeks and the postpartum constipation/hemorrhoids were a nightmare!

Trying to squeeze back into my jeans a week after delivery was laughable. I don't know why I thought my body, which had changed significantly over the nine months it took to grow a human, was supposed to just go back to "normal" once you had the baby. My tiny apartment bedroom was crammed with Nick's crib in one corner and my single bed in the other. I remember quietly trying on all my clothes during his nap to see what I could actually wear because I'd be damned if I was going to go back to wearing maternity muumuus!

With no car and a small welfare check to live on, I kept my spirits high by taking Nick for long walks in the neighborhood, cleaning, and re-cleaning my apartment. Meanwhile, I had friends over several nights a week and, at the time, we were all smoking like chimneys. Yikes! I cringe now over poor baby Nick's lungs being exposed to that horrible air for any length of time. For the most part, I was conscious of being a responsible young mother, but there were definitely moments when I was clearly more teen than mom.

Surprisingly, Rob was usually patient with early fatherhood. Prior to Nick's arrival, I definitely worried about how Rob would react to a crying baby. He was a charismatic, caring individual but Rob was not ready to become a dad. Yet there were plenty of moments when I could see and feel he did love Nick. However, beyond the basics of care, he really didn't know how to build an emotional bond; he wanted to be in control of both Nick and of me.

Between the time Nick was born and his second birthday, my relationship with Rob became very tiring for me. Rob wanted to dictate where I went, who I talked to, and who I saw. He grew suspicious and I felt he was always checking on me. Not that I was doing anything wrong—all I had time for was mothering and work. The longer it went on, the more I knew I had to break up with him. My gut felt he would not be kind about it or take the news well so I spent months thinking about how I could break away and still keep him in Nick's life.

What I didn't consider was how Rob would take out our break-up on Nick for years to come. And what I didn't understand was how Nick could be so loyal to Rob, not telling me what he was experiencing at his father's hands, even though Nick and I had great rapport and discussed lots of difficult topics as he grew up.

When Rob and I broke up, I was working for a company that developed strip malls in the Midwest. Receptionist was my title; in addition to patching through phone calls to the dozen or so employees, I typed letters and reports, copied blueprints, and made coffee among other tasks for several men in the office. Overall, I liked the job and most of the people. The location was convenient to my parents' house where Nick stayed during the day and it paid enough to keep us off welfare.

I missed Nick and looked forward to leaving work on time, picking him up, going home, making dinner, and relaxing during the evening. Even though Rob and I had broken up, he took Nick several nights a week, and I had extra time to myself until we met so Rob could pass Nick off to me.

One evening I was getting ready to leave for the day when Jeff, one of the guys I worked for, brought a letter and a long list of names to me. He said he needed it typed and envelopes addressed in order to mail the letter. I looked at the letter: It was a message to his golf buddies promoting an outing a few months away. He gave it to me and headed back to his office to make a phone call. Even though it was 4:55 p.m. and I had already shut down my typewriter for the day, I decided to go ahead and get it done quickly. I typed up the letter and the envelopes and took them into his office, quietly laying them on his desk so he could proof them when he was ready. Then, I put on my coat and grabbed my purse and walked toward the door; I glanced at the clock on the wall, it was 5:15 p.m. — time to get Nick and go home to make dinner.

The next morning, Jeff called me into his office immediately. I could tell from his tone of voice and demeanor he was extremely unhappy. We had always had a good working relationship. Walking behind him down the hall, I tried to figure out why he was so obviously bent out of shape.

He pointed to a chair, where I promptly sat. He went to the other side of his desk, sat down and asked, "What the hell do you think you're doing leaving the office before finishing your work? *Who do you think you are?!*"

"It was a letter to your golf group," I replied. Shocked and immediately defensive, this was all I managed to say.

"I don't care who the letter was to, I asked you to do it," he lectured. "I wanted the letter mailed out last night as you left work. I needed you to get it to the post office, so it could make the last pick up."

I stared at him, thinking, "You've gotta be fucking kidding me. Really??"

"You are the hired help, remember?!" He continued his tirade. "That means you don't leave until the work is done!"

At this point, I was tearing up because I was not expecting this kind of humiliation, neither in that moment nor in any other, and I couldn't believe, based on prior experience with this man, he was berating me about a letter regarding a golf outing that was weeks away.

Jeff told me to get out of his office and never do anything like that again or I would be fired. Calmly, I walked out of his office, tears streaming down my face and went directly into the bathroom. A friend of mine, a senior secretary, came in behind me because she'd passed me in the hall. "Sometimes these guys can be real assholes," she told me as she hugged me. "They think just because they have a title behind their name, they can treat us like shit."

I pulled myself together and went back to work as if nothing had happened, but the relationship I had with Jeff was never the same. He had made me feel an inch big when it was completely unwarranted and unnecessary. I was a twenty-one-year-old single mom, trying my best to make a living and take care of my responsibilities. I worried all the time about what would happen if I lost my job. The humiliation of being on welfare when Nick was born never really left my mind, even though it wasn't public knowledge.

My anxiety about never having enough money was quelled by getting a couple of credit cards that allowed me to buy cute clothes and go out to eat more often than I should have. It made no sense, intellectually and financially, and I knew it, but I kept doing it, telling myself I'd do better next month.

"Money doesn't grow on trees," I heard as a kid. "It's hard to come by and can be taken away at any given moment." These phrases quietly reverberated in my mind. Finding security for myself and my son was understood, on a deep level, to mean I couldn't do it on my own and needed someone else to support me.

Interlude

LIVING LIFE THROUGH THE LENS OF MY GREATEST FEARS

Entering into my adult life, while I projected to the outside world that I had my shit together, beneath the surface I unconsciously lived according to the following limiting beliefs:

> I'm not worthy of being heard.
> I need to perform for love and approval.
> I can't trust myself.
> I'll never be good enough.
> I don't make healthy choices.
> Be careful with money.

In part two you will see these themes play out over and over again in the woman, wife, and mother I was, as recounted through various milestones and events: our wedding, having more children, moving, and my on-and-off professional life. These beliefs are especially evident throughout my marriage and parenting.

These limiting beliefs literally guided my life until I woke up to them a few years ago.

What is a *limiting belief*, anyway?

A limiting belief is an often-subconscious concept you have about yourself or your life. The belief holds you back from being who you truly are, in other words, your highest, most authentic self. It keeps you from being *you*. These beliefs infect and inhibit your relationships, your career choice, where you live, how you dream, and how you parent.

Everyone takes on some limiting beliefs about themselves, often during childhood–even if you have the world's most "woke," conscious, intentional, emotionally healthy parents. The limiting beliefs you developed may not be the same as mine, yet every one of us has experiences that make indelible impressions on who we are.

To be clear; I did not share stories from my childhood in these pages to throw my parents under the bus. In fact, I have a wonderful relationship with both of my parents and believe they loved me very much (and still do). I had a very normal childhood. I know it was likely much more pleasant than a lot of other kids experienced. If you're a parent too, you know how easily we lose patience at least occasionally. We have bad days. Some parents, often those raised with physical discipline, will spank or smack their kids, believing this is part of child-rearing. Spanking was a very acceptable discipline method when I grew up in the 1970s. Many adults saw nothing wrong with using their parental authority to hone their kid's behaviors. I have intentionally never lifted a hand to my kids because I remembered how deeply it affected me on the rare occasions I experienced it growing up.

My parents weren't unusually cruel or punitive by any means. They raised me the best they could with what they knew, and as a result of their own life experience. They raised me the way they had been raised, through the traditional, dominant parenting paradigm: *Children are to be seen and not heard. Children are to respect their elders. A child's behavior is more important than the connection.* For generations, we've been parenting over our kids, not with them.

The practice of conscious parenting wasn't well-known, let alone openly talked about, by generations previous to mine. I was in my forties before I even heard the term *conscious parenting.* Honestly, I wish I'd had some inkling as to the importance of working through my childhood shit before my kids were born, or even while they were little. I would have avoided projecting my own personal insecurities and parenting fears onto the kids I've raised. But, because I've done the work needed to uncover, process, and shift the limiting beliefs that were unconsciously placed on me as a child, my kids have a fighting shot of raising their children without projecting generational baggage onto any future grandchildren.

In the coming pages, you will witness how often I abandon myself; you will understand how many times I shut my mouth in the name of keeping the peace, choosing to "be a good wife and mother" because that's what I learned growing up and because I was too afraid to express who I really am. This is what we do as mothers who were raised to be *good* girls. Maybe you will see some of yourself in my story. If not in the experiences themselves, the feelings you absorb through my words will likely resonate with some part of your journey. So many women I work with are nearing the end of the intenseness of their parenting career. They feel empty and alone because they've put everything into their children, neglecting to continue growing their own interests and learning new skills outside of those that come with motherhood. Then they wake up one day in mid-life and wonder who they are and what they're going to contribute to the world aside from the wonderful children who have come through or to them.

Raising You

THE LIMITING BELIEFS THAT PLAYED OUT IN MY LIFE

HE'S THE ONE

After I broke up with Rob, Nick and I moved across town to an upper flat on 69th Street in Wauwatosa which gave me the opportunity to strike up a friendship and then romantic relationship with my husband, Tom. Tom lived in the tiny third-floor studio of the townhouse next to my flat; we literally shared a driveway.

I actually knew Tom from childhood. Our families had shared that same townhouse before eventually moving to other homes. Tom's parents had kept the townhouse as an investment property and now their oldest son, Jim, and his wife, Kim, lived there as newlyweds. Tom, a young bachelor, rented the third floor. Over the years, Tom's parents and mine had remained close friends; we would see his family from time to time, but it had been several years since I had actually seen or spoken with Tom.

To say it was love at first sight might be an overstatement, but not by much. Tom was handsome, hardworking, and often mowed my lawn without asking. It felt kind of like living next to Prince Charming! So, when I needed a date to our company's Christmas party in December 1990, I knew exactly who I wanted to ask. One evening, after procrastinating for a few weeks, I took a drag off my Virginia Slim Extra Long Menthol Light™ cigarette, followed by a large swallow of

Beringer White Zinfandel, and called Tom to ask him out.

The Christmas party went well and we began to date. Since Tom was new to going out with someone who had a three-year-old, there were some bumps and hesitations at first. We talked about his worries, worked through the kinks, and within six months he proposed! Neither of us was really looking to get married at that point in our lives, but it just kind of came together. Our parents were ecstatic, of course, to become in-laws on top of being great friends.

After our engagement in June 1991, we experienced a lot of grown-up change and commitment in a very short period of time. First, Tom and I got married in May 1992. Then we bought our first home just three months later in August. The housing market was strong. Financially, things fell into place, and we bought a four-bedroom bungalow in Wauwatosa, a short drive from the area where we'd been renting. Nick was in five-year-old kindergarten when we moved into our first house. He continued to attend the public elementary school where he'd attended four-year-old kindergarten. I had left the receptionist job and started as a full-time administrative assistant with the Guardian ad Litem Division of the Legal Aid Society. The position gave me an opportunity to work for eight attorneys and five social workers who represented abused and neglected children in Milwaukee County.

It was mind-blowing to learn firsthand the devastating effects parental abuse could have on children and families. Our office worked towards reuniting families after the parents were redirected through parenting classes, or served jail time, or had been treated for substance abuse. The kinds of abuse to which some of the kids were subjected was often shocking, not to mention the number of kids in the system! Our office itself was located inside of the county's juvenile detention center; sadly enough, many of the kids who came through our office grew up to become juvenile offenders and spend time in the detention facility.

The third big event of the year happened at Christmas, when Tom and I announced we were pregnant with our first child!

My pregnancy with our first baby went along without a hitch and, in late July 1993, I went on maternity leave. This was the first time in Nick's life I'd gotten to temporarily become a stay-at-home mom and we were all excited to become a family of four. Allen-Michael arrived on August 7, 1993 at 9:20 a.m. after about twenty minutes of pushing. We'd talked about stopping at a garage sale on the way to the hospital — thank God we didn't because I would have given birth on the sidewalk! Though there were moments during my pregnancy when I knew Tom was nervous about becoming a dad so quickly after we married, he was obviously very proud of his firstborn son.

Any anxiety I might have had about bringing a sibling into Nick's life (after six years of being an only child) quickly vanished when Nick came home from this weekend visit with his dad. When he held Allen-Michael for the first time, Nick grinned from ear to ear; he was so excited to be a big brother!

CALM

About three weeks after Allen-Michael was born, Nick started a new school for first grade. After kindergarten ended, Rob insisted Nick go to the Catholic grade school he attended (the one I had also attended before my family moved to the lake house when I was in fourth grade). Rob didn't practice the religion of his childhood but, for some reason, he really wanted Nick to go to school there; he was even willing to pay the tuition. Since it was a natural starting point for Nick to switch schools, I was on board. The school was on the way to my job when I returned to work so the convenience was a plus, too.

The first two or three days went okay. I could see Nick had some nerves but that's to be expected when starting a new school and I was able to help him work through the transition. However, by the second week of school, it was clear every morning was gearing up to be a battle and I was not sure who was going to need more strength: me to get Nick to school, or him to endure the school day. Each morning he would get up, cry, and repeat, "I don't want to go to school!" I had to physically put him in the car, strap Allen-Michael into his baby seat, drive to school with a screaming child (which could have been either Nick or Allen-Michael – or both at once – on any given day). Then I had to drag a crying, kicking, and screaming Nick across the school parking lot while cradling a newborn, amid stares from other families on the playground. It got so bad that the principal would meet me at the school door and take Nick from there.

To say it was both exhausting and heart-wrenching to have to go through that scene each morning is an understatement. After a few weeks of dealing with Nick and the beginning of the school day battle (and Tom trying on and off to help), I'd had it. I asked Rob to come over and take him to school. By this time, I was knee-deep in newborn sleep deprivation because Allen-Michael was up a couple of times a night to nurse and I was completely out of ideas to get Nick to cooperate. I desperately wanted to figure out a way to turn things around for him. I knew Nick was quickly getting a bad reputation at his new school, both with his teacher and his classmates, due to the early-morning dramatics that often lingered throughout the day. He was such an unhappy little boy during that time.

The first morning Rob came over to get Nick, he'd quietly cried but didn't get as worked up as usual. I knew it had to be because he knew his dad meant business and there was no point in trying to get out of going to school. I was silently pissed that Rob was not going to see Nick's usual behavior about going to school, but also relieved to have the burden off my chest for the day. My plan was to have Rob take Nick each morning for a few weeks until I could recoup and find the courage to try again.

That first morning Rob showed up to get Nick and take him to school was also the last. Thirty minutes after they left, Nick was back on the doorstep with Rob standing behind him, fuming and yelling, "The kid refuses to go to school!"

I admit, I was annoyed at Rob for not trying harder, for not getting help from the principal like I had been doing every day, but Nick was crying so hard I just let him inside the house and told him to go to his room. I got Allen-Michael settled in for his morning nap before softly knocking on Nick's door and letting myself in. He was lying curled up on his bed with his back to me, I could tell he was still crying. I sat down on the bed next to him and put my hand gently on his shoulder, all the while worrying how I was going to parent him through this issue he was having. He seemed to jump a bit when I went to rub his back; he told me to stop doing that because his back was hurting. *That's odd*, I thought. So I asked him if he'd fallen or gotten hurt in some way as I began to lift up his t-shirt and saw black and blue marks on several areas of his back!

Oh my God! Rob had beaten him! Oh my God! My mind was screaming! I knew he had a short temper and could be physically aggressive with me (which is ultimately the reason I broke up with him), but I had no idea he would ever resort to beating Nick! I was sick about it! With tears in my eyes, I hugged Nick and asked him to tell me what happened. He shared a little of the story, saying his dad was angry at him for crying at school and spanked him.

Spanked him?!?!

My energy shifted. I left Nick in his room (thinking he still needed punishment for disobeying at this point), and walked outside where I could have some privacy. I immediately called Rob. My momma bear instinct came out. "What the fuck were you thinking?!" I roared into the phone. Basically, Rob's response was that Nick deserved it for being disrespectful and defiant. He had zero remorse. I still carry guilt about making the decision to involve Rob in the situation; yet I know I truly was at a loss as to what to do, worried Nick would never make friends, and concerned Nick's teacher didn't like him.

I honestly don't remember how we managed to get past the early morning drama, but it eventually worked itself out, somehow. Obviously, I never asked Rob to take Nick to school again. Shortly thereafter I went back to work, leaving my mom to care for Allen-Michael.

A few years ago, I asked Nick to think back to that time in his life and tell me, if he could, why he'd had such a hard time going to school every morning. "Hell, Mom, I thought you were going to take off on me," he said.

I had worked full-time for most of his young life and he was so happy and at peace having me home with him for the first few weeks after Allen-Michael's birth, he didn't want to leave the house for fear I would disappear. The years of anxiety and drama through which I'd put my parents, especially my mom, came back to haunt me.

During the weeks of turmoil as Nick adjusted to his new school, Allen-Michael was a thriving baby, so incredibly content and happy just to hang out with us. Rarely did he fuss or cry, even though a lot of the time during those first few months I was a basket case trying to help Nick enjoy school. Allen-Michael has since remained low-key and extremely good-natured.

LEAVING HOME

At the beginning of 1995, Tom decided to take a national sales position with the outdoor advertising company he'd worked for since graduating college. This meant we had to move from Wisconsin to Northern California. For me, the move was somewhat exciting, but mostly nerve-wracking to think about. I had never lived far away from my parents and I relied pretty heavily on their presence in our lives. In addition, both Tom and I had siblings and family we were fairly close to and heading out West meant we'd be counting on each other a great deal more for everything.

Of course, the new position required Tom to start right away, leaving me in charge of two boys (who were eighteen months old and seven years old). It was stressful. I was still working, it was a bitter cold and snowy winter, and I made several trips to and from California so Tom and I could find a new house. There was no way we could have made the transition without my mom's help with the kids!

The move also meant I had to hire a lawyer, again, to negotiate a new child support and visitation schedule with Rob. As you can imagine, it was not pretty. I was adamant that Nick finish out second grade in Wisconsin, which was about the only thing upon which Rob and I agreed. Rob wanted Nick 50% of the time which made no sense to me at all because, though he loved his son, I knew he didn't really want to be a parent 50% of the year. He just didn't want me to have Nick. The stress-filled legal battle was his way of getting back at me for being happily married and having an opportunity to move far away.

Months of trying to negotiate a fair agreement through our attorneys led to Rob and I working with a mediator and then landing in a courtroom in front of a judge with a less-than-secure agreement. The judge didn't know us; he only knew what was on the paper in front of him and what our attorneys presented to him. He didn't care about who our son was or how splitting our parenting would impact his life.

To say no one won in the end and Nick was, in fact, the biggest loser in this case would be the truth. Going through the legal proceedings concerning Nick was the hardest part of the move for me and not the least bit his fault. In addition to leaving all that was familiar to him, this move meant the poor child was going to have to start a new school, again. Nick was roughly the same age I was when I left the same beloved school he was leaving. Memories of how poorly I'd dealt with a big move and starting a new school plagued me, even though my parents had only moved me thirty minutes away while Nick's move involved a cross-country flight and leaving one parent behind. I'm sure both he and Allen-Michael could feel the disruption in my energetic response to life as we started this new chapter.

Even though Rob and I couldn't get along, I knew Nick having his biological dad in his life was necessary. I tried very hard not to speak ill of Rob in front of Nick. But there were times it was extremely difficult since, in our legal proceedings, he fought dirty and openly criticized me when Nick was within earshot. In my opinion, Rob asked for additional time with Nick because he knew the more overnight visits he had, the less child support he had to pay. He hated paying me money. Though I absolutely believe he loved Nick, I don't think he had any idea how to be a good parent and he hated feeling like the loser in this area of his life.

Six months later, when Nick was almost eight and Allen-Michael was nearly two, the boys and I watched the moving company pack up our home and put it on a large semi-truck headed west. Then, because of the new visitation order, I had to turn around and say goodbye to Nick until August. This move put him into the hands of his dad who worked full-time. This meant he would be spending forty hours a week with his paternal grandmother; while she enjoyed Nick's company, she didn't often leave the house. In contrast, I was finally going to be a full-time, stay-at-home mom since we were losing the world's best and cheapest sitter—my mom.

We lived in California two years to the day! Two *stressful* years to the day. California is a beautiful state, and the weather beats the hell out of Wisconsin, but housing is much more expensive. The beautiful, character-filled, old bungalow we'd bought in 1992 for $190,000 in Wauwatosa, Wisconsin sold for a few thousand more when we left in 1995 but we ended up buying a brand-new tract home that was quite a bit smaller for

$250,000 in California. The new house didn't even have window sills!

Tom's California commute to and from the office was a lot longer with intense traffic, which played a role in his mood when he got home each night. Although his parents lived five hours south of us, they were really the only close family we had nearby. Most of our neighbors were transplants as well, so we did make some friends; but none of them were as strong as the ones we'd grown up with and left behind in Wisconsin.

The first November we lived in California, I worked a part-time job in a local department store because we didn't have enough money to buy Christmas gifts for the boys. The second Christmas, I worked at Target for the same reason. On the nights I was scheduled to work, Tom and I would meet in the mall parking lot. He'd take the kids back home, feed them, and put them to bed while I pulled a shift from 6-11 p.m. or midnight. It was enough to provide Christmas gifts, which was wonderful, but nothing else about the job or the holiday season those years was joyful.

Tom took a management position with his same company back in the Milwaukee office in June 1997. For years afterwards, he gave me crap about it being my fault we ended up back in the snow and endless winters. He really liked the atmosphere in California minus the commute and money stress. I knew I had a lot to do with his decision to head back to our home state. Professionally, Tom was intrigued by the idea of going into management as opposed to being in sales, and I just plain wanted to go *home*. When school let out for summer, my mom flew from Wisconsin and we put her on the plane with the boys while Tom and I drove across the country with our belongings in a U-Haul™. Next stop: Delafield, Wisconsin. Delafield was a super-cute, tourist town midway between Milwaukee and Madison. We were buying in Lake Country—a bigger house with a much bigger yard! I literally ended up sending Nick to the same public school I attended (and ran away from) so many years earlier!

Right after we moved back to town, my younger brother, Paul, and Tom's only sister, Therese, got married. They'd actually started dating the night of our wedding five years earlier. It was a great evening, in part because I got to stand up at the altar with my husband again. I indulged my romantic side all day, thinking about our big day five years prior, and how much we'd accomplished and weathered since that momentous occasion. On the other hand, it was also a day to remember for another reason. I spent most of the day trying to quell an awful migraine while pretending to have fun. The next morning, I bought a pregnancy test and confirmed my suspicions: hello, family of five! Happy fifth anniversary to us!

COURAGE

The next few months flew by. Between raising two kids, keeping up a large home, and being a supportive wife, there was never much time for me. However, that changed, unexpectedly, one morning in November 1997, four months after Paul and Therese's wedding. Nick was in fourth grade, Allen-Michael was in preschool, and on top of the usual daily mom/wife duties, I was back in school, taking some general education classes at the community college.

By all outward appearances, my third pregnancy appeared to be humming along without issue until I began leaking fluid one morning. At first, I chose to ignore it but by the second day, I was beginning to panic. Thanksgiving weekend was approaching and I couldn't deny the issue any longer. Never having had the problem before, I finally decided to call my obstetrician. I hated to disturb him and his family on Thanksgiving. My doctor told me to take it easy, eat some turkey, and come into the office the next day. So, I did.

After running some tests, he determined I was, indeed, slowly leaking amniotic fluid. He admitted me for a night of observation that turned into weeks. Suddenly, I had lots of time on my hands, thrust out of the regular routine of being at home. Tom and I were told I would likely deliver the baby within a week of the rupture since it was difficult to replenish amniotic fluid, even with a lot of water intake on my part. The other problem was I could potentially develop an infection, which would force an emergency delivery.

We learned this news when our baby's gestational age was 26 weeks and 2 days. During the first of several in-depth ultrasounds, we found out he weighed 1 pound and 8 ounces. As the measurements were taken, Tom and I were given a laundry list of potential birth defects that could result from a delivery this early. Phrases like *immature lungs, cerebral palsy,* and *brain damage* were used to caution us. I looked across the room from the examination table to see Tom crying. I knew I would be able to find a way to handle whatever was thrown our way with this baby, with trepidation of course, but I also knew, in my heart, Tom would have a much more difficult time coming to terms with a child who was born with birth defects. It was one of the very few times he allowed himself to express his fear, and was vulnerable enough to respond through the tears he let me see.

From November 28, 1997 to January 8, 1998, I lived in a hospital room, spending most of that time in bed. During my stay in the hospital that entire holiday season, Tom had to take over at home. Fortunately, his parents came into town from California and stayed several weeks, and of course my mom was nearby with her helping hands, as well. I never saw our Christmas tree, but I did order all the boys' presents through catalogs that year. And then I made Tom bring them to the hospital for a wrapping party so I felt at least a little bit involved in everything going on outside of my 10' x 12' prison.

On Christmas Eve, the nurse rolled me down the hall in a wheelchair and I was allowed to spend an hour with ten-year-old Nick and four-year-old Allen-Michael, Tom, my parents, and my grandparents to celebrate the holiday. We ate sub sandwiches and my mom's wonderful Christmas cookies. When everyone left to carry on their usual traditions, I quietly lay in my bed rubbing my belly, telling the little boy inside my body about what Christmas would be like next year.

Forty-one quiet nights I waited. On the forty-second day our baby would no longer call my belly his home. In the middle of a classic Wisconsin snowstorm, Brigham Richard, weighing a whopping 4 pounds and 7 ounces, arrived just in time for dinner. The early afternoon of January 8, when labor started again for what I felt like was the hundredth time since the end of November, we all knew there was no stopping it. I was prepped for a C-section, and Brigham was born moments later! Although he had some minor breathing issues at birth, he was healthy. He was able to come home within a week of his arrival, which was wonderful since I desperately wanted to be home with Tom and the other boys.

I was incredibly grateful Brigham was physically and mentally healthy! I know if he had ended up with challenges, I would have risen to meet them. Even at that point in my life, I was letting faith, calm, and courage navigate my journey. There were many lonely moments during my long stay in the hospital and plenty of time for me to reflect (which, as a mom of two and one on the way, I would never have had otherwise). I knew I wanted to be the best mom I could be to the baby that was about to arrive, so I was preparing myself for the worst—which meant being brave and vulnerable enough to step into what it would be like to parent a child with special needs.

Both Nick and Allen-Michael were really happy to have me home and to get back into a routine. Sure, they enjoyed their grandparents being around, but there's nothing like Mom being home. I spent the next few years focusing on our family of five, trying to be the best wife and mom I knew how to be, while getting an associate's degree in interior design.

PATIENCE

I actually got pregnant on our tenth anniversary in 2002; we were on almost the same pregnancy timeline as Brigham, our fifth anniversary gift. Maddux was due mid-February as well. It's funny (or maybe not), but I don't remember much about my pregnancy with Maddux. I remember clearly how it ended, but not so much the 34 weeks beforehand. I am pretty sure it was because I was busy building an interior design business while trying to stay on top of three boys, my husband, and the house.

During my twenty-sixth week of pregnancy, I stopped long enough to wonder if I'd get through it without a repeat performance of what had taken place five years earlier. But, thank God, the week came and went without incident. On Christmas Eve 2002, we hosted both of our immediate families and their children, along with our aunts, uncles, and cousins. My Aunt Sue and Uncle Jim were visiting from Phoenix that year. While they were in town, my aunt began having some serious health problems; sadly, it turned out to be her last Christmas as she passed away months later from cancer. I am so thankful we were all able to be together for that final holiday.

Filled with loved ones that snowy night, our house was super festive. We were fortunate enough at the time to have a huge kitchen that could accommodate everyone. Living in Wisconsin meant the season was marked by the usual snow and bitter cold, but we compensated for the bleak weather with lots of new toys and great holiday treats!

After winter break, just as the boys were getting back into the school routine, I woke one morning and began to make the bed. Whoosh! I felt a sudden gush of fluid. There was no mistaking the issue, this time. Tom was already at work, so I scrambled to call him, the doctor's office, and my mom to take care of Brigham.

"Baby number four is on the way today!" I announced.

Laughing at myself, I ran around the kitchen with a big towel stuffed between my legs, making bagged lunches for Nick and Allen-Michael so they could get on the bus for school. As they left through the front door I yelled after them, "You'll have a new brother or sister by the time you get home today!" Tom and I knew it was another boy, but we had tried hard to keep the gender a secret from everyone else.

It was a beautiful winter morning, bright sunshine and nearly 60 degrees, almost unheard of for January in Wisconsin! I knew with the way my water had fully broken and mild contractions set in there would be no six-week hospital wait this time around. A short time later, I arrived at St. Joseph's Hospital. St. Joseph's had long been a part of my family's lives. My dad had been born at the same hospital, then me, and it was where I had delivered my other three boys. I hobbled through the hospital lobby with a new, semi-dry, towel shoved between my legs, knowing I was, once again, in a place where the doctors and nurses had seen it all; I was just another lady showing up to deliver her baby.

By lunchtime, we welcomed Maddux Anthony, born via C-section, weighing four pounds, eight ounces. He was a week later in gestation than Brigham had been. If he had waited just one more day, the two of them would share a birthday. Since I had delivered early, I missed Brigham's fifth birthday party at Chuck E. Cheese. He wasn't too happy about that but eventually forgave me.

Four days after Maddux's birth, our drive home from the hospital was much different from the ride there. On January 7, I'd worn a sweatsuit to the hospital, enjoying the unseasonal sunshine, but when we went home on the 11th, it was gray and bitterly cold. The following months were rough; it was miserably cold both inside and outside of our house. Living on a lake, though beautiful in summer, felt extra frigid in winter as the view from every window was a huge sheet of ice and the wind fiercely whipped off the lake. With a new baby, I was, again, sleep-deprived in addition to trying to keep up with four boys, Tom, my interior design clients, and of course, managing the house and cooking.

By the time Maddux was two months old I found myself in the pediatrician's office three times in one week. I've always been the kind of parent who favors a "wait-and-see" approach, meaning I don't rush to the doctor's office every time my kids sniffle or have a fever, but this was different. Maddux's incessant crying every day was both physically and mentally exhausting. The third time I showed up that week our pediatrician said, "Mrs. Muench, I believe you have a colicky baby on your hands."

A *what?!?!* I had briefly heard of – and very much feared – colic before Nick was born. I was scared I would be in a tiny apartment far from my parents with a constantly screaming baby. Although Nick definitely had his moments and his share of long nights (as the other boys had as well), he was never colicky.

Our pediatrician explained colic is defined as episodes of crying lasting three hours at a time, three days a week or more, for at least three weeks in a row. Bingo! That explained Maddux to a tee. *Okay great, so I've got a colicky baby; now what do I do?!* Sitting in the small examination room, with Maddux in my arms, I was bewildered as to how to help him. The doctor told me to swaddle him snuggly in a blanket (*I've done that*, I thought) and whisper "Shh" quietly in his ear (*I've done that, too*); unfortunately, the colic would just need to take its course. "One day, likely by four months of age," she said, "he'll just wake up and seem like a brand-new child you don't recognize."

I burst into tears. That was the only time I've ever cried in front of a pediatrician. Here I was with my colicky fourth son, I was freezing my ass off in the midst of my least favorite season, mentally and physically exhausted, being told there was no miracle cure to get this kid to stop screaming. *Oh my God*, I thought. *I'm going to lose my shit right here.*

But I didn't. Like so many other times in my life, I just sucked it up as so many other mothers do. I found the strength and the patience to bear the challenge. I didn't ask for help, for someone to take over so I could just get a little peace, because I didn't feel worthy of asking.

Somehow, by the grace of God, I managed to get through the next several weeks. Then one morning, exactly as the pediatrician promised, Maddux woke up and acted like a totally different child. That day, and for several days afterward, Tom and I looked at each other and silently mouthed, "Who the hell is this kid and where did Maddux go?"

Every once in a while, motherhood gives you a break.

DENIAL

Over and over in my life, I've felt it necessary to show up as whoever someone else needed me to be rather than honoring my own thoughts and feelings. A situation that occurred in 2004 illustrates this point perfectly! Tom and I were in the process of moving and I was a few months pregnant with baby number five. We had not talked about the pregnancy much because we were busy packing the house and caring for our four other children. The day before the moving van was scheduled to arrive, I noticed I was spotting. Being the eternal optimist that I am, I didn't think much of it. It had never happened during my previous pregnancies. *Plus*, I thought, *we're in the middle of a move, so there's no time to stop and worry about something like this.* But as the day wore on and the spotting not only continued but got worse, I decided I should at least call my doctor. I called and the nurse asked me to come in the next morning. "Tomorrow is our moving day," I told her.

"You should come in anyway," she instructed.

So, the next morning, I left Tom with the kids who weren't in school and went to the doctor. They put me in an exam room where I waited a long time. Which happens, right? Finally, the doctor came in to discuss my symptoms. Then, I waited, again, as the doctor left to get a nurse to do a sonogram. While waiting, I worried about Tom trying to navigate watching one-year-old Maddux along with the movers. I knew my husband well; anxiety presents as irritation, snippiness, and shortness of temper in him. He was likely getting very edgy back at home. Finally, the nurse completed the sonogram and the doctor returned to talk with me.

"There's no indication the baby is alive," the doctor informed me, then continued to tell me what I could expect to happen as I miscarried over the next forty-eight hours. "I'm sorry," she said before leaving the room.

My cell phone rang as the door closed behind the doctor. It was Tom.

"Hello," I answered.

"Where the hell are you?!" he asks, exasperated.

"Where the fuck do you think I am?" I asked. "Apparently, I am having a miscarriage, but I'll rush right home and get on everything that needs to be done today, honey. Don't worry."

And that is exactly what I did. I just kept going *because who am I to stop and actually acknowledge what I am going through?* That would mean I mattered and I need to be the on-top-of-it, organized, supportive wife and mother of four. Don't get me wrong. I love my kids and my husband. *But I didn't love myself enough to demand having a say in my life and to acknowledge my feelings.*

Not only did we complete the move that weekend, as I dealt with sporadic, horrific cramping, but we also attended the wedding of a young woman I babysat when I was a teenager and she was a little girl. Tom and I changed out of our grubby moving clothes, dressed up, and had a lovely dinner at an upscale private country club. All evening, I worried over whether my body would betray me and I'd bleed all over the dance floor. To everyone else, we just looked like any other couple there to celebrate like all the other guests.

I have only myself to blame for each and every time I chose to go along with life and the situations in my marriage to keep the peace. I learned early on to not make waves or create conflict. But why?!

Projecting this behavior onto my mom because that's what she modeled for me – and my grandmother for that matter – would be accurate, in part.

But it is not the full story.

Raised like so many kids were for so many generations, I was taught, from the beginning of my life, to behave in ways that made those I loved most accept me and love me back. I was afraid of being abandoned. My actions and behavior were directly related to my sense of love and security, to my deep fear of abandonment. This is what we teach our kids on a very deep level when *what they do* is more important than *who they are*. And THIS is why adults today have an incredibly difficult time acknowledging their true feelings and working on themselves. Looking within ourselves would mean having to admit we have betrayed ourselves over and over in the name of earning love and acceptance from others. Instead, it's easier to say we're failing as parents because we're being too soft on our kids rather than controlling them better as was done in previous generations. Yet, even with the knowledge of this generational pattern, despite every intention not to perpetuate those patterns, and in consciously practicing not doing it over the past decade of my life, I've done the same thing to my own kids!

GRACE

As the spring of 2004 progressed, we settled into our seventh home, which was definitely my favorite! Still in Delafield, but now off the lake, we bought a two-story colonial on a beautifully landscaped one-acre lot. It was everything I'd ever dreamed of in a home. I continued to do some design work and my mom or the older boys took turns watching Brigham and Maddux so I could meet with clients. In 2001, I had started my own business, From House to Home Interiors, which was perfect because it allowed me to do something creative that I loved, on my own schedule.

In the beginning, I wanted any client who would work with me, so I took every job that came my way. But, as time went on and I had a few successes under my belt, I learned a great deal about people. I connected really well with some, while others were very stressful to work with on a project. Being a wife and mom to four boys was enough stress at times. I didn't need to add difficult clients. By nature, I am a people pleaser; I take it very personally if someone is unhappy with my work. Within only a few months, I realized that there are just some people in the world who aren't happy, and love nothing more than to blame others for their unhappiness. I quickly learned to identify those people and to say, "No, thank you." The more kids I had, the fewer jobs I was able to accept. Parenting has always been my number-one priority. As time went on, the jobs I did take were with people who were fun to work with and who truly appreciated my design expertise.

One of the most enjoyable yet challenging parts about being a designer was and is being able to marry a couple's decorating tastes. Sometimes, I felt like more of a therapist than a decorator! Helping two people compromise their vision in order to accomplish their design goals is a real art. However, I found nothing more satisfying than to hear a client say, "I LOVE the way this room turned out!" I didn't go into the business for the money (much to my husband's chagrin), though it was not that we didn't always need it. I was in it for the satisfaction of knowing I'd helped someone create a home where they loved to live.

In the fall of 2004, I was busy working with several clients so I don't even remember finding out I was pregnant—I do, however, remember the battle Tom and I had, once again, about finding out the baby's sex. We'd fought about whether or not to have an ultrasound when I was pregnant with Brigham and Maddux; both times, I won. I intended to have it my way this time as well. I understood Tom's point of waiting until the birth because there are so few fun surprises in life — I really did. But it never outweighed the fact that, in my heart, I'd always wanted a baby girl. As much as I loved each one of the boys and wouldn't trade them for anything, my heart's desire was to have a daughter.

Maybe it was because I'd enjoyed such a close relationship

with my own mom and wanted to recreate that bond, or maybe it was the super cute little dresses that fueled my desire. Whatever the reason, I wanted the opportunity, after four boys, to have a girl. Thus, I needed to find out ahead of time so I could move beyond the disappointment I might feel if I didn't have a girl. Having an ultrasound before the baby's birth would help me prepare to be excited on the big day and not the least bit disappointed. In the end, I won (which, again, rarely happens).

"It's a girl," the ultrasound technician announced the news I'd dreamed of hearing.

I have to admit, I cried right there on the exam table while alternately saying, "Shut up!" "Really?!" and "Are you sure?!" like a hundred times. Honestly, I don't know for whom I was happier: me or my mom! On one hand, it was so hard to contain the excitement and not stockpile tons of super cute baby girl dresses, tights, and hair bows as we awaited her arrival. But on the other hand, there was a lot to keep me busy with four boys now aged sixteen, ten, six, and eighteen months, not to mention a husband, a house, and a handful of design clients.

Fortunately, this pregnancy progressed smoothly, which was a relief after the miscarriage I had earlier in the year. The knowledge of two previous early births was important as we got into the third trimester and, although I had a new doctor, she was fully confident in taking care of me and the baby if that were the case again. Because Tom and I had decided this baby was going to be our last child and my tubes would be tied after the C-section was complete, I wouldn't be delivering at St. Joseph's. As a Catholic hospital, St. Joseph's did not offer tubal ligation procedures; thus, we needed both a new doctor and new delivery space this time.

Baby number five, my girl, was due on Mother's Day 2005. Nevertheless, in the early morning of Sunday, April 3, I was startled awake by a strong contraction. Wide awake, I lay still in our bed for a few minutes trying to process what had happened and to see if anything else was going to follow. I didn't feel anything else, but couldn't sleep, so I tiptoed downstairs to watch television and wait. A little while later, I felt a mild contraction and then a few minutes later, another. At 3:30 a.m., I called the doctor and told her what was happening. She was on call at the hospital that night and asked me to come in for observation.

I called my mom and asked her to come watch the boys, even though it was a Sunday morning and Nick, a teenager, was driving at this point. Then I crept upstairs and woke Tom, telling him we needed to go to the hospital. "Shut up!" he said, in a tone that conveyed his stop-kidding-around-this-isn't-funny mood. "I've been up for hours already," I responded. "The doctor wants me to come check into the hospital." He got up and, while he showered, I finished packing a bag, then greeted my mom at the door.

We arrived at the hospital, the early spring day dawning as we checked in and got settled. I was feeling hopeful and excited as the sun rose! Time passed slowly while I was hooked up to monitors and very little, if anything, happened. After a few hours of no real contractions, my obstetrician decided it was time to release me. There wasn't enough labor activity to consider delivering. When she left the room to complete the necessary paperwork for release, Tom turned to me.

"See," he said, "I told you the baby wasn't coming today."

F-you, I thought, staring at him. That was probably one of the most hurtful things he could say to me in that moment.

He left to get something from the car to pass the remaining time before we could leave and go home. Once he walked out of the room, I began to earnestly pray, which was totally unlike me. I asked God to please, please let me meet my baby girl today. I begged all the deceased female relatives I could think of, including my grandmothers and my aunt to help me out. (It just seemed appropriate to ask the females.) Then, a few minutes later, the oddest and most wonderful thing happened—I began to have contractions. Strong ones, close together! The monitor tape was frantically going up and down! The doctor returned with the discharge paperwork and some instructions for me.

"I don't think I'm going anywhere," I announced. "Take a look at the print-out on the monitor." Seeing that labor had picked up, she agreed that, at 36 weeks, it was time to deliver.

Tom returned to the room and found me bent over the side of the bed as the anesthesiologist prepared to administer an epidural. If ever I doubted there was a God who could conjure up miracles (and I did), I was now a true believer!

Our daughter, Mia Louise, weighing 5 pounds even, arrived at 12:37 p.m. on April 3, 2005. It was a sunny, warm Sunday and she was a beautiful gift from God. My baby girl arrived with a twinkle in her eye. Mia is the most light-hearted, loving child I know. She doesn't walk; she skips, and she always has.

Mia was baptized a few weeks later on Mother's Day (her original due date) and her seventeen-year-old brother Nick was her godfather. During the church service, I had an overwhelming sense of pride and peace looking at what I perceived as the complete picture of my wonderful, idyllic family.

I had no clue what was coming.

LIFE IN MOTION

Tom is the hardest working man I know. It's the first character trait that comes to mind when I think of him. He is the second of four kids in his family and he worked to pay for his Catholic high school tuition by mowing lawns and shoveling snow. Tom paid for college the same way, as well as taking on additional jobs like becoming a parking lot attendant each morning before his classes began.

He worked for the same outdoor media company from the time he graduated in 1989 until June 2017. Tom was in local sales, national sales, management, and then returned to local sales before he left the company. He has always taken providing for his family very seriously. I know it hasn't been easy; in fact, being the sole source of income for a wife and five kids has been incredibly stressful at times. While I have worked outside the home on and off throughout our marriage, the bulk of my contribution has been running the house and taking care of the kids.

In December 2006, Tom found out the sales manager in his company's Dallas office was being promoted to the East Coast and he wanted to put his name in for the job in Dallas. At that point, we'd been back in Wisconsin for a decade and he felt, in order to move up in the company, he needed to change markets.

Moving across the country to Texas concerned me for a lot of reasons, not the least of which was that Tom had not always been happy in his sales manager role. This is not to say he wasn't good at it; it just seemed there was little control over the financial outcome, and a great deal of pressure when you counted on a dozen or more salespeople to pull their weight and produce the magic numbers the bosses wanted every year. Dallas was a much bigger market than Milwaukee and Tom knew going in that there would be even more pressure to perform along with the potential for making a better living. This translated to more stress at home, knowing Tom as well as I did after almost two decades of marriage.

Another concern I had was how the kids would cope with such a big move. When you've got a houseful of kids, ranging in age from toddler to newly-graduated high-schooler, there are a lot of moving parts and personalities. Each of them presented different situations to navigate as we prepared to move.

On his eighteenth birthday, Nick decided to move out of the house; he lived with his dad about twenty minutes from our home. He'd graduated from high school in the spring and was attending classes at a local junior college while working at our town's main grocery store.

Allen-Michael was months away from graduating middle school and had been with the same group of kids since kindergarten. Even though he'd always been laid back and a go-with-the-flow kind of kid, the adjustment he'd have to make going into a new high school with a new group of kids worried me most. Admittedly, memories of having to make friends as the result of a move during my own childhood impacted my anxiety about this for him.

Brigham was in third grade. He was very well-adjusted and had a great group of friends. Our free-spirited child, I thought he would do okay with a move to a totally different environment.

Maddux and Mia were four and two, respectively, so I wasn't as concerned about their reactions. As long as we were together, I knew they would thrive no matter where we lived.

For me, the move also meant giving up the design business I loved and had grown for six years. I loved bringing people's dreams and vision to life through color, pattern, texture, artwork, and cool knick-knacks. Helping people redecorate a room or their entire home has always meant a lot to me. In fact, it was often so much fun, I thought it was ridiculous that people paid me to do it! Over the years, I developed some great relationships with my vendors, as well as my clients, and I knew it would be challenging and require a lot of energy (not to mention time) to build a new clientele in a market I didn't know.

As if those reasons weren't enough, our entire extended family was in Wisconsin; we had an amazing group of friends; and we owned a beautiful home. It was a lot to leave behind! On the upside though, I absolutely hated long, cold winters and moving south would give us an opportunity to leave them behind. I was also excited because it would be an adventure. I had never been to Texas (actually never even thought about Texas, to be honest). And, of course, there was the chance this position would be the one that would bring Tom contentment and happiness.

Weeks of interviews later, Tom was chosen for the promotion, which meant, worried or not, we set the wheels in motion for months of stress as we prepared to head south and begin yet another big change! Babies and moves, babies and moves, babies and moves—there was a definite pattern in our lives between 1993 and 2007!

TRANSITIONS

Tom accepted the new position just before Christmas 2006. We spent the winter and spring of 2007 finding a place to land in Texas. Of course, the company needed him in Dallas right away, so I was left to sell the house, wrap up my business, and prepare the kids for the transition.

In mid-January, Allen-Michael, Brigham, and I flew down to meet Tom. We decided it was important to take the two boys with us to Texas so they could better understand where we would be moving. We wanted them to see what would be the same and what would be different about living in Texas as opposed to what they'd always known in Wisconsin. The first marked difference was the weather. It was cold, blustery, and snowy in Wisconsin the morning we left for Texas, but when we walked out of the Dallas-Fort Worth airport, it was sunny and 55 degrees. Now, that made me smile!

Over the following months, I took three additional trips on my own to Texas to look at housing. The real estate agent who was recommended to us through Tom's company turned out to be a bigger liability than asset to us. She lived in a very upscale community and would only show us homes in that area, which would have been great if we had a million-dollar budget. But we didn't, and her attitude about showing us what we could afford in a different area was not the least bit helpful in making this move with four kids. She kept pushing the wealthier areas of town and it was not at all who I was or wanted to be.

Finding a home in Texas was a very frustrating process. On the weekends Tom didn't fly home to see us, he drove to other areas of the Metroplex looking for options. The situation became alarming when our home in Wisconsin sold; the buyers wanted us out fairly quickly and we had no place to go. I called Tom in a panic as the house in Wisconsin was about to close. The movers were asking me whether they needed to pack our things for delivery or for storage and I didn't know the answer!

Tom ended up finding a brand-new home in a new development in a town I hadn't seen before. But it did have the sixth-best high school in the state that year, according to a local publication, D Magazine. The house itself was located on Lake Geneva Court. Since Lake Geneva is also a lovely tourist town in southeastern Wisconsin, I decided the coincidence was an omen that we should live there.

Though our new home wouldn't be ready for us to move into until the first week of May, we had to be out of our Wisconsin home by mid-April. The logistics put a lot of stress on both Tom and I but we tried not to show the kids, which I thought we did a good job of at the time. Remaining calm and single-minded, in order to create as smooth a transition as possible for the kids while also figuring out how to get a million details taken care of before leaving the state, was my focus. Meanwhile, I was preoccupied with my own worries about going to a home, city, and school district I knew very little about and had not yet seen, adding to the already stressful situation. I didn't have the time or the emotional bandwidth to consider my feelings or sadness about leaving people, places, and familiarity I knew behind. Tom was living in a one-bed, one-bath apartment in Dallas, knee-deep in work. After our house in Wisconsin sold, the kids and I stayed at my in-laws' condo for a week before leaving town with my mom to cram into the apartment with Tom for a cozy ten days.

During those first days in Texas, I drove Allen-Michael and Brigham thirty minutes each way to their new schools until we could get our furniture and belongings out of storage, and move into the new house. By the time all was said and done, we had lived out of suitcases for more than three weeks. It felt like the world's longest move!

The house Tom found and bought on Lake Geneva Court was 2,000 square feet larger than our home in Wisconsin, and felt much more formal. Hand-scraped hardwood floors were all the rage so we had those on the first floor, along with a grand spiral staircase in the two-story foyer. When I walked through the house for the first time, I had a hard time believing we were actually going to live in something so big and fancy, especially coming off of ten days in a one-bed, one-bath apartment!

Allen-Michael and Brigham attended the last few weeks in their new Texas schools. This was, in part, because I learned from my experience with Nick so many years earlier that even a few weeks in a new school at the end of the year would be better than arriving during summer break and not knowing anyone. Not knowing anyone meant a lot of boredom and nobody wants bored kids, right?

Moving to Dallas meant we left Nick behind in Wisconsin, which was hard. There was really no reason for him to come along since he had started community college, had a girlfriend, and had a job. But I felt a mix of guilt and sadness about being so far away from him, even though he wasn't living with us the few months before we decided to move because he felt we had too many rules. Apparently, things were easier at his dad's house. Because he lived only a few minutes away, Nick would often come for dinner or to spend the night. Our move made continuing those visits impossible, of course.

The night before we left Wisconsin for the big move, the kids and I were staying at my mom's house and Nick came over to say goodbye to all of us. He took time to read bedtime stories to Maddux and Mia and gave us all lots of hugs. Looking back, I didn't realize how hard our move to Texas was on him. During those months after he'd moved out of our house, I tried to tell myself everything would be okay. He was with his dad, in school, had a job and a girlfriend; he was becoming an adult. After all, I was a mother by his age and lived on my own in a tiny one-bedroom apartment. Nick was doing just fine, I told myself, figuring things out while making his way in the world. I was wrong. And in my gut, I had a nagging feeling I was bullshitting myself, but I kept doing it, anyway.

The cul-de-sac we moved into had a few families already living there, but none of them had a child as old as Allen-Michael. I knew it was important to get the boys invested in their new state quickly, so sports were a natural first step. Initially Allen-Michael and Brigham were in constant, daily contact with their friends in Wisconsin (as was I). There were definitely some comments made by each boy about how much they wanted to go back. It was a rocky start but, again, they are both pretty easygoing and in time, thank God, they adjusted to the move across the country.

STORMS AHEAD

In January 2008, several months after our move to Texas with the kids well on their way to being adjusted, my maternal Grandpa passed away suddenly, at the age of 94, from heart failure. Grandma had died several years earlier and my mom had taken care of my grandpa since then, ensuring he had nutritious meals to eat, great- grandkids around to make him smile, and even some wood-working projects to keep him busy. My grandpa and Nick shared a birthday, so their bond was extra-special. When Mom was making the funeral arrangements, she wanted all of us there, so she scheduled a memorial service two months later in March during our Spring Break to accommodate us traveling north. Even though it was a somber occasion, everyone was excited about the trip. We packed up the kids and drove for sixteen hours to be a part of the celebration of Grandpa's life. Of course, it also gave me an opportunity to see Nick, which made my heart happy. He'd only come to visit us once in Texas since we'd moved.

Before our visit ended, I wanted to spend some time alone with Nick. Shortly after we moved to Texas he moved out of his dad's home and into an apartment with a friend. Nick told me he'd moved out because living with his dad was unbearable. He was still in school, working, and had the same girlfriend. Something told me there was more going on, though. We went to lunch and Nick admitted he'd been having a tough time emotionally. He felt depressed and had taken an online mental health quiz. He believed he was suffering from symptoms of obsessive-compulsive disorder (OCD). Nick was vague about exactly what was going on, but the more I listened to him, the more I could tell something was definitely up; my mom instinct was rightfully alerted.

As our lunch continued, I expressed how bad I felt we were so far away. But once he told me what was on his mind, he appeared to relax a bit, and then reassured me he'd be okay. Things were going fine with his roommate, Mark, and his classes and his job were good as well. I suggested he see a counselor who would be able to help him with his thoughts and feelings. I also offered to contact our insurance company as soon as we got back to Texas for a list of in-network therapists so he could be evaluated for depression and have some unbiased emotional support. My commitment seemed to both make him happy and relieve him as we finished an overall uneventful lunch together.

From my perspective, Nick and I enjoyed a close relationship and talked easily with one another. We never argued or fought; often, during middle school and high school, he came to me to talk about various situations in his life, including his dad. I knew it wasn't easy for him to go back and forth between our home and his dad's while he was growing up. Over the years, Tom and I observed that, when he returned from a visit with his dad, it took Nick a day or two to get back into the swing of things at home. That's not unusual for kids who split time between parents. And although Rob and I had our challenges, I always encouraged Nick's relationship with his dad and didn't spend time or energy criticizing Rob, especially in front of Nick. To do so would not have been right or the least bit productive. By the time Nick began high school, I didn't have much contact with Rob because Rob had given Nick a car against my wishes. The only time Rob and I saw one another was when we both attended parent-teacher conferences.

As the years passed, on occasions when we were both in the same space, I noticed Rob's demeanor was off. At one high school parent-teacher conference, in particular, I remember an intense alcohol smell. During conferences, I explained to a number of Nick's teachers his dad and I weren't together because, quite frankly, I didn't want them to think I was married to him. Rob was loud and somewhat inappropriate in these conversations and it made me feel uncomfortable.

Nick and I talked about it sometimes; he acknowledged his dad drank quite a bit. But Nick made it sound like it wasn't really a big deal. By the end of high school, Nick didn't spend much time with Rob; at least, he wasn't following the visitation schedule put in place when we moved back to Wisconsin. When Nick did go for the weekend, he often slept over at friends' houses because we didn't allow him to do that when he was with us. Because we remembered the kind of behaviors we participated in when we were in high school, Tom and I decided on a no-sleepovers rule after Nick turned sixteen. Nick didn't like the rule, but we felt it was an important boundary. Being the first child, Nick did not like more than one rule Tom and I had, but that is typical for a teenager! We were trying to negate some of the antics we pulled during our own youth.

When we got back to Dallas after the memorial service, I called our insurance company, as promised, to get a list of counselors within twenty minutes of Nick's apartment. Right away, I called Nick with the information and encouraged him to make an appointment as soon as possible because it could take a few weeks to get one. During the following weeks, I made sure to call and check in with Nick several times. He started to answer sporadically and sometimes it took him a few days to return the call when I left a message. A few times, I checked with Rob to see if he'd heard from or seen Nick when he did not return my calls. Quelling my mom instinct, for the most part, I chalked Nick's avoidance up to his being busy with school and work or to his being too lazy to pick up the phone and call his mom. The conversation we had over lunch was still in the back of my mind and I was somewhat concerned about him. When we did talk, though, he often reassured me everything was okay and he was feeling somewhat better. During this period of time, Nick had dinner with my mom at least once a week and, afterward, she reported to me about his demeanor, behavior, and their conversations, so I felt another layer of comfort. It seemed Nick was just going through the normal bumps that come with growing up and living on his own.

After several more reminders from me in the months

following our trip to Wisconsin, Nick finally did make an appointment with a therapist who then referred him to a psychiatrist for antidepressant medication. Nick began seeing the counselor for talk therapy. Still concerned, I told myself I was reasonably comfortable with these new measures and everything would be okay since he was now actively working on his mental health and had family support nearby.

THE TRUTH

My anxiety level hit the roof when Nick called on a Tuesday evening the first week of May. "Mom, I need help," Nick said when I picked up the phone. "I don't remember the last three days of my life and I've just spent the entire day recovering from a blackout." As I worked to process this greeting he continued. "This isn't the first time it's happened. I'm scared."

"Okay, honey, tell me what's going on." I was shocked, scared for him, and felt guilty about being so far away. I listened to Nick tell me what had really been going on the last several months. On top of the blackout from which he was recovering, he was failing school and knew he was about to lose his job, as well. I could no longer deny the feelings I had been suppressing and reasoning away. There was a bigger problem than I wanted to admit and Nick was now verbalizing it through the phone line from miles apart.

As he spoke, I realized he'd only been partially honest with me during our lunch in Wisconsin. Though I was hearing this information for the first time, my gut said Nick's depression and OCD were exacerbated by the cycle of binge drinking. According to Nick, when he moved into his friend Mark's apartment, his drinking escalated pretty quickly because there was not anyone around to keep tabs on the two 19-year-olds. Based on what he'd told me, when Nick moved out of his dad's house, I understood why he wanted to move in with Mark. He didn't say his dad's drinking had gotten out of hand; he blamed their rift on the unreasonable expectations his dad had about keeping his room spotless, demanding that he help around the house, and his dad's inability to control his temper. I knew firsthand how angry and unreasonable his dad could be, and totally understood why Nick chose to move in with a friend.

In hindsight, I was totally naïve, thinking Nick could make it on his own at nineteen since I had made it on my own at the same age (with a newborn, no less). But Nick and I had essentially grown up in two very different environments and it was obvious, now, things were not going well for him. The more he shared, the more apparent it became he was scared shitless about the direction his life was headed.

Generally, I am pretty even-keeled. Even in emergencies, I'm good at keeping myself together and working toward a solution without panicking. You could say I have an *everything-happens-for-a-reason* demeanor and consider those words ones by which to live. Trying to keep my head straight, I quickly calculated the options, which were few, considering we lived 1,200 miles south of the situation at hand. Nick coming to Dallas wouldn't be an option in Tom's eyes, especially with all the problems we were learning about. Tom cared about Nick, but the desire to protect himself and the rest of the kids from dealing with what might be something big, emotional, and uncertain wouldn't fly. So, knowing my mom was five minutes from where Nick was staying — she already fed him once a week, and she lived alone since she and my dad were divorced — I told Nick I would call Grandma and ask if he could go there.

Unsurprisingly, my mom said yes; she's always been there for me and she lives to serve others, so Nick moved what little he had into her guest room the very next day. They sat down and talked about house rules (no alcohol) and chores he would be responsible for while living with her. I was, of course, incredibly grateful she was willing and able to take him into her home.

As it turned out, his moving into her guest room gave us an almost immediate and clear (albeit scary) picture of what was going on in Nick's world. Since he'd been fired from his job for excessive absences, he intended to begin looking for a new one. Together, we decided it was best to put school on hold since summer break was approaching. He was failing because he couldn't concentrate, and we all agreed he needed some focused time to work on his mental health.

Nick moved in on a Wednesday, and the following Sunday was Mother's Day. I called my mom early Sunday morning to share my Happy Mother's Day wishes with her, knowing she was headed to work. I was hoping to get a card in the mail from Nick: you know, the once-a-year I Love You Mom in written format. It didn't arrive in Saturday's mail, but on Sunday I received an e-card from him. Nick knew I was very worried about him after all he'd told me earlier in the week, so I thought it was somewhat selfish on his part not to at least pick up the phone to say hello. This was yet another example of my ignorance and naïveté about addiction.

The next afternoon, Mom called. I was surprised since we usually only talk about once a week. She didn't want to alarm me, but needed to share what had happened with Nick. My mom, like me, possesses a low-drama persona, so I knew she wasn't blowing things out of proportion.

The night before, she'd come home from work around five o'clock and Nick was in his room with the door closed. Mom knocked to see if he wanted dinner but got no response. She tried again a while later with no response. Following her instincts, she opened his door. Nick was passed out drunk in bed with his bottle of antidepressants next to him. Scared, she immediately tried to get him to respond; he barely moved or made a sound. Not knowing what to do next, she called my brother, Paul, who lived five minutes away, and asked him to come help her. While waiting for my brother, mom continued attempting to get Nick to respond. By the time Paul arrived, she had gotten Nick to sit up in a chair and he was talking a little more. Together, they decided it would be best to take him to the emergency room for an assessment. Mom and Paul managed to load him into the car. Once they arrived at the ER, Nick was given IV fluids and the doctor on call encouraged him to check out Alcoholics Anonymous. The situation obviously unnerved both my mom and me. At this point, I was freaking out about how quickly this situation was getting out of control; I was also really worried about my mom being involved to this extent. There wasn't much she would not do for any of her kids or grandkids, but this was not at all what I wanted for her.

Mom handed the phone over to Nick and he and I talked for a long time. Nick understood what he had done was incredibly dangerous. He knew he'd scared us with his lack of control around alcohol. If there's one thing I've learned about my Nick during the last several years, it is that he doesn't drink to party or socialize, although I am sure that's how it started. He drinks to medicate himself from feeling anxious, depressed, and worthless. During his treatment, I found out he had been drinking alcohol and smoking pot since he was fifteen years old. Trouble sleeping was a problem he mentioned to me on occasion during high school and, apparently, he abused Nyquil, marijuana, and occasionally alcohol to help him relax enough to get some rest from his ever-racing mind. I knew Nick also had some trouble with anxiety and depression over the years. Splitting time between his dad's house and ours was no treat. Unfortunately, like many other kids whose parents didn't stay together, there was no way around the dynamic.

A handful of times when Nick was in high school, Tom told me he thought Nick was taking liquor from the cabinet above the refrigerator. Thinking of my own teen years and how I'd snuck some brandy or scotch from my parents' cabinet at times, I was always the one who confronted Nick; he relentlessly reassured me he was not taking liquor from our cabinet. Honestly, I believed him for a number of reasons: 1) because I thought we had a relationship built on honesty, trust, and mutual respect; 2) because, at times, I felt Tom was a little jealous of the relationship I had with Nick and maybe wanted to create an issue where there wasn't one; and 3) I didn't want to believe there was a problem—the latter being the most dominant reason.

Tom was so adamant he started marking the liquor bottles and checking them often. He even took pictures of the way they were placed in the cabinet. To this day, I don't know whether Nick knew this, or if he continued to take the liquor and found a way to compensate for the diminished reserves. Regardless, during high school, the tension between Nick and Tom grew and then exploded on Nick's eighteenth birthday, when Tom directly accused Nick of stealing alcohol and the two nearly came to blows. In the end, Nick backed down and simply walked out of our house, saying he would move in with his dad.

Like most mothers, my momma bear side comes out and my loyalty leans to my kids first. That doesn't mean I think my kids cannot make a bad choice or do any wrong. And it does not mean I will stand in the way of their being accountable for the consequences of their choices. It does, however, mean I believe the kids who have come through me are gifts. I have a responsibility to love them unconditionally and to look out for their best interests while giving them space to grow and mature into morally-responsible adults. Parents are meant to be guides and role models upon whom kids can lean. When we don't fulfill that role, they will wave the bullshit flag with their words and behaviors to let us know we are not in sync.

In case you wonder what kind of example have I been for my kids with regard to my own alcohol use, from the time I was nineteen and on my own, I have had a glass of wine and a bowl of snacks (either Fritos or Cheetos in earlier years and Healthy Pop popcorn more recently) every night around 10 p.m. before I go to bed. No lie, I have done this since Nick was a baby. I never drink and drive (because I did that shit in high school, and I realized one day how stupid it was). If we are out for an evening with friends, I usually have two or three glasses of wine. On occasion, I may have had a few more when we were younger, but I learned pretty quickly that too much wine gave me a hangover, which meant I didn't have the energy to parent the next day.

When I was growing up, my parents had a similar habit, only earlier in the day. When my dad got home from work at five o'clock, they enjoyed a cocktail or two each night while discussing the day's events before dinner. I'm sure there are some people who would jump to judge or criticize my end-of-the-day ritual. The way I look at it, some people take a bubble bath, read a good book, or listen to soothing music. Me? I watch HGTV, drink my wine, and eat my snack.

As for disciplining Nick during his teen years, his sixteenth birthday exemplifies our approach. For his sixteenth birthday, Nick's three best friends and fellow band members came for a sleepover. In addition to our home, there was also a small cottage on the property down near the water. Nick's friends came over to practice music, eat pizza, and hang out together to celebrate Nick's day: nothing too crazy.

After they ate dinner, Nick let me know they were going to walk to a local park. Around eight o'clock, I got a phone call from a police officer who said he'd just left Nick and his friends. The officer happened upon them smoking cigars at the park and gave them a warning for underage smoking. This shocked me because I had no reason to suspect Nick would ever smoke. As a matter of fact, for years he had condemned his dad's habit and tried, off and on, to get him to stop. The officer explained he'd only given the boys a warning because they cooperated with him and no one had any prior issues with the law. He also said the fine for underage smoking was $360. That was a lot of money to us and I felt Nick was very lucky for not getting ticketed. I thanked the officer for calling and put down the phone.

Five minutes later, the boys walked in the door, and Nick immediately told me what had happened. Not quite knowing how to handle the situation (this was my first teenager), I asked the other boys to call their parents to come get them. I told Nick I was very disappointed in him and we would talk about his punishment in the morning. I needed time to think things through and discuss it with Tom.

Ultimately, Tom and I decided the best consequence for Nick would be for him to take the next $360 he earned from his part-time job at McDonald's and donate it to the police department to use for smoking prevention programs. This would take him a while to accomplish because he only worked 10-15 hours a week at minimum wage. Nick was saving for a new guitar, so it also meant delaying his goal. We thought this was fair and would, hopefully, deter Nick from continuing to smoke. We also implemented the no sleepover rule at this time; it was the last sleepover he hosted or attended when he was at our house.

I think we made the best decision, given what we knew then. Nick was not happy about the consequences, mainly because the other parents just gave their sons a short lecture, if that. Like I said, it was my first go-round with a teenager. I remembered how I felt and behaved in high school and tried to be relatable, yet not like a friend, to Nick. That sleepover experience was the only brush with the law we had with Nick during high school. Yet, looking back, it's easier now to see how there were little things going on that we just dismissed as just part of growing up.

ROUND TWO

My mom had booked a flight to visit us in Dallas several weeks before Nick moved in with her. Given the current circumstances, we were both anxious about his being alone in her house while she came to see us. If he drank while she was there, what would he do when she wasn't around for a week? I didn't want her to change her plans because she really wanted to see the kids, and, quite frankly, I really needed a hug from my mom. On the plus side, Nick continued to see his counselor weekly and said he felt doing so was helping. In the end, to quell my growing fears, I decided to fly to Milwaukee without telling Nick and spend the week with him while Mom was at our house in Dallas. She was happy to get some quality time with the kids. My plan didn't leave much time for she and I to visit; however, we both felt more comfortable with this new arrangement.

Mom arrived on a Wednesday morning, but I wasn't scheduled to leave for Wisconsin until early Friday morning. Maddux was graduating from preschool and I didn't want to miss his cap-and-gown ceremony on Thursday morning. Trying to balance my attention so each of the kids felt loved and seen and had their special moments celebrated during this time was difficult at best. Like so many previous situations in my life, I just kept going without paying attention to my own needs, wants, or feelings.

When I got to the airport to pick up Mom, she told me she was so glad I'd decided to book a ticket to Wisconsin. Just before leaving that morning, she found a nearly-empty bottle of vodka under the sofa in her recreation room. She poured it out and left it on the kitchen counter with a sticky note that read, "Please don't do this to yourself, Nick. I love you, Grandma."

Nick called me shortly after Mom and I got home from the airport. First, he asked to speak with his grandma and made her swear she wouldn't tell me about the bottle. (Obviously, he wasn't thinking that would literally be the first thing out of her mouth when she sat down in the car.) He promised her he wouldn't drink again while she was gone. His vow did nothing to relieve the anxiety Mom and I felt. To say we were extremely stressed in the time between that phone call and my arrival at her house in Wisconsin would be an understatement. Promising my mom that he'd be good, Nick then asked to speak to me. I just popped back on the phone like nothing was out of order, asking him random questions about his plans for the next day or so. I didn't want him to have any clue I was coming to town. I wanted him to believe I had complete confidence in his ability to spend his days looking for a new job just like he told me he was going to do.

Thank God I had my mom to talk with during this time; we counseled each other through a lot of emotional challenges during Nick's spiral with alcohol addiction. Neither of us could fathom how quickly Nick's behavior had spun so out-of-control. Many days, I walked around feeling like I'd been punched in the stomach. While I always thought I was hiding it well from the other kids, I now know, even if we aren't talking about our problems directly in front of our children, they *feel our energy* and know when something is really wrong. My heart ached for Nick; he was torturing himself through uncontrollable binges with vodka. His struggle brought to light the dark realization of how deeply sad and depressed he must have been to drink himself into oblivion. And I had no idea how to stop it! Then there was the question of where he was even getting the alcohol—he was a minor, after all.

During these difficult months of uncertainty about Nick, I held all of my outward emotion in check until the kids were asleep. All my tears were shed once I could hear Tom snoring quietly beside me. As time went on, I felt I had to share some information with Allen-Michael and Brigham because they were old enough and aware enough to see I was "off." But at this point, as far as they knew, I was just going to Wisconsin to spend some quality time with their big brother.

Thursday morning's ceremony at the preschool was a tough one to get through without tears. Maddux had his special preschool graduation celebration. But while I tried to focus on the joy of seeing what a big boy he was becoming, I was very distracted wondering how Nick was doing (assuming he'd continued to drink, would he get behind the wheel of a car?). So many scenarios and what ifs were flying through my mind when all I really wanted was to focus on my cute, loveable five-year-old in his miniature cap and gown. When Maddux received his diploma and walked across the stage, I kept thinking it was just yesterday when Nick did this. *Where did I go wrong? What the hell was going to happen next?!*

Later in the afternoon, I put Allen-Michael in charge while Mom and I went for a pedicure and out to dinner. I'd made the appointment earlier in the week because I knew we'd have limited time together and we'd both be in worry-mode. Our girls' night out was a much-needed diversion. Earlier that day, I had called Nick twice to check in with him and got his voicemail both times. This only heightened our anxiety but we tried not to show our unease. Surprisingly, I was actually able to force myself to relax and enjoy both the pedicure and dinner with Mom. We tried hard to talk about things other than why Nick wasn't returning my calls.

Before we got home from our evening out, I tried reaching Nick one more time. At this point, it had been a full twenty-four hours since our phone call, and I knew he'd been drinking even before Mom left town. Trying not to freak out, I told my mom I was really worried and was going to ask my brother to go over to her house and check on him.

Unfortunately, my brother wasn't able to go. He was in charge of his three kids and, obviously, I wasn't going to ask him to drag them along, not knowing what he might find when he arrived. So, I busied myself with putting my own kids to bed. By 8:30 p.m., with the kids settled in or doing their nightly reading quietly in their rooms, I was beside myself and went to

Mom's room. I told her I wanted to call my dad and have him go over to her house and check on Nick. She agreed it was a smart next step.

My dad knew a little about what was going on with Nick, but I'm sure my phone call was a surprise to him. He was at the ballpark watching a Brewers game when I called. Despite baseball being one of his favorite pastimes, he answered the phone and agreed to leave the game and check on his grandson.

The time between the end of our phone call and him calling me back felt like the longest forty-five minutes of my life! My mind kept churning images of Nick lying across the bed on his back, blue-faced and wide-eyed, vomit coming out of his mouth from asphyxiating himself. And the thought of my dad finding him and what that would do to him sent me right over the edge. I kept praying, *please, God, let everything turn out okay!*

Dad finally called back and told me he'd gotten into Mom's house only to find Nick in bed, and his girlfriend next to him trying to take care of him. He was passed out and she told my dad she didn't have any idea what to do. I am sure she was relieved to see him and hand off the job of watching over Nick. My dad was able to get Nick on the phone and, through his tears, he said, "Mom, I am so sorry. I know I told you I wouldn't do this while Grandma was gone. I told you that you could trust me and that I was feeling better." Through my own tears, I told him how much I loved him, and that I had a flight booked for early the next morning and I'd help him figure things out. I was obviously relieved Nick was still breathing, but panicked and stressed at trying to figure out how I was going to be able to help him get through this time in his life. My dad stayed with him all night and until my brother picked me up at the airport and then dropped me off at my mom's house the next day.

When I walked in the house, I sat down next to Nick on the sofa. I opened his hand and placed a palm-sized smooth rock etched with the word "HOPE" into it. I had intentionally bought it at the spa the day before and brought it to give him something concrete and meaningful to hold onto. "Nick, without HOPE you have nothing," I told him. "You must always have hope in your heart." We hugged and cried. "I'm here to help you," I continued. "Please work with me and trust me."

Next, I called our insurance company and explained the situation. They referred me to a detox facility near Mom's house that also had an outpatient program. All of these events happened so quickly it was hard to know where to go and to whom to turn. I had no experience with alcohol intervention and didn't have any friends who'd been through it, either. We immediately went to the detox center and spent the next few hours waiting, filling out forms, and learning all about detox and outpatient therapy programs. Nick was willing to sign himself into forty-eight hours of detox, so I left alone. I was incredibly grateful knowing he was in a safe environment for the next two days. I slept very soundly the nights he was there; it was only then that it dawned on me how much I'd needed the physical and mental rest.

When I visited Nick the next morning he said, "Do you have any idea what it means to me that you are sitting in this room with me right now?" I tried to be very clear, using lots of eye contact, about how much I loved him and how scared I'd been for him the last few weeks. We talked about everything that was going on in his life. I told him how much I thought he needed to go to AA regularly and see his therapist more often. By this point, I understood he needed to share his feelings so they wouldn't build up and drive his anxiety level so high that the only way he knew how to cope with it was to drink until he passed out.

When I had walked in the door and saw Nick for the first time, I observed he had a black eye and a banged-up arm. He didn't remember what had happened to him. A few days later, while I was scouring my mom's house for bottles of alcohol, I noticed a shattered banister at the bottom of the basement stairs. I questioned Nick about it and, after thinking a minute, he said he vaguely remembered falling down the stairs. *Oh my God! My son could have tumbled down the stairs and died in the rec room!* He seemed remotely concerned about this when we put two and two together but was not nearly as freaked out as I was about the whole thing!

Three days later, Nick was released from detox and he had an appointment with his therapist, which I attended with him. During our days together, I felt like we had a lot of good conversation and it was great to have some one-on-one time with him. We also found an AA meeting and he filled out several job applications. At the end of the week, I needed to return to Dallas. Mom would be flying back into town the next morning. Nick did fine the one night he was alone and my mom returned to a happy, "normal" house guest.

If only it would last.

HERE WE GO AGAIN

A few days after I left Milwaukee, Nick was hired for one of the jobs he'd applied at while I was in town. Sam's Club wanted him as a stockperson. He attended AA intermittently and continued to regularly meet with his therapist. Since I was a total newbie in the world of addiction, of course I was concerned, but I'm also an optimist so I felt reasonably sure he was doing okay. Optimism or denial? The weeks ahead would paint a clearer picture.

Being 1,200 miles away from Nick was hard. We talked on the phone several times a week, and he still lived with my mom who had allowed him to stay, contingent upon his following additional house rules she set. One of those rules was that he eat dinner with her any night he didn't have to work. Nick's food intake was sporadic and he didn't make great choices. He pretty much lived on Red Bull, which I am 100% certain exacerbated his anxiety and shitty sleeping schedule. Of course, my mom always took care to ensure there were lots of his favorite, healthier foods around the house to subtly coax him into better eating habits.

For a few weeks, everything seemed to be moving along fine and on an even keel. And then one July afternoon, out of the blue, Nick's girlfriend called me to say she thought I'd want to know he'd been drinking and hadn't made it to work that day.

She also shared he'd missed a few shifts lately and she was worried about him again. I told her how much I appreciated her phone call and let her know, straight up, she didn't deserve to be going through this with him. It was obvious at this point there was a definite pattern emerging with Nick's self-harming behavior and I thought she should value herself enough to consider taking a break from dating him. Looking back, I think it was probably the wrong thing for me to say at the moment, to meddle in their year-long relationship, but she called me and I wasn't about to pussyfoot around and not be honest with her. As much as I love my son, she did, indeed, deserve better treatment from the relationship than she was getting. He cared a lot about her but he wasn't in any shape to be in a relationship. I ended the call by telling her if she ever needed to talk to please feel free to call me. I didn't know her all that well, but knew she didn't have a very close relationship with her parents and she had a lot of drama in her friendships as well, from what Nick said.

Apparently, as soon as we got off the phone, she decided to tell Nick what I'd said and just a few minutes later I had a very angry, drunk son yelling at me. Of course, I was fielding these phone calls while trying to remain present in mothering my four younger children who were all home. Calls with Nick, when he was drunk, were never fifteen-minute affairs. I quickly learned how impossible it was to try and keep what was happening with Nick a complete secret from Allen-Michael and Brigham. The other two kids were too young to understand why I'd be on the phone for hours, but it was totally out of character for me and the older boys knew it.

I had no choice that afternoon but to basically put Allen-Michael in charge while I locked myself in my bedroom closet so I could talk in peace. I wanted to give Nick my attention, too. Juggling five kids' needs can be tricky, and this was definitely one of those moments. I am sure there were times during the months Nick's drinking was escalating when the rest of the kids wondered what the heck was going on. Mom taking sudden trips and talking on the phone during dinner hours or bedtime routines was not normal behavior for her at all.

After an hour, I hung up on Nick as he was mid-sentence because I finally realized you can't reason with someone under the influence of alcohol. Our conversation was going nowhere and he wasn't open to any of the suggestions I was making for getting more help. He wanted to vent and be right about everything rather than listen to me. When I cut the line, I didn't even know where he was calling me from, whether he was at home or would be driving a car somewhere after I hung up on him.

Several hours later, my mom called (it was now mid-bedtime routine for Maddux and Mia). She said Nick really wanted to talk to me. So, once again, I obliged. I asked Tom to take over the kids and I planted myself on the front porch. In the dusk of a hot, Texas summer night I spoke to my inebriated twenty-year-old son. He ranted, he cried, he burped, he drank, he urinated off my mom's patio and, all the while, I listened. I told him I loved him. I told him I knew better things were in store for him but he needed to dig deep and to find the courage to face his demons sober. I got off the phone about midnight, emotionally and physically drained. Mom and I spoke before I hung up the phone and she said she thought she could get him to go upstairs and sleep it off.

My poor mom: I absolutely hated this for her!

I stopped Tom before he went to work the next morning to thank him for taking over with the kids and to fill him in on the night's events. I told him something needed to change. Nick needed more help than he was getting through weekly therapy and occasional AA meetings. Tom had no idea what to do next and reminded me we weren't in any financial position to keep flying up to Wisconsin every time Nick decided to get drunk. Clearly, I knew that but in case I forgot, he was there to remind me.

Later the same morning, I called our insurance company to get their input on the situation. They gave me the name of several detox and outpatient facilities in our area. I then called my mom and told her I was going to book a ticket for Nick to come down to Dallas the very next day. I just couldn't keep putting her in a situation where her grandson was drunk and she was having to take care of him. Just like that, the following afternoon, we picked up Nick from DFW Airport. The two of us immediately drove forty minutes to an insurance-approved treatment facility where I had set up an intake appointment.

What I found absolutely mind-blowing about his alcohol binges was how relatively quickly Nick could recover from the amount of alcohol he consumed. He could drink a bottle of vodka like it was water and still walk and talk! Doing something like that would have made me incredibly sick or possibly even dead! Nick experienced mild handshakes and high anxiety for a few days after binging, but he made it sound like it was manageable. Nick looked and spoke completely normally less than two days after several hours of binge-drinking hard liquor then becoming unconscious.

During the previous months, I learned Nick was an intelligent, nice, obedient young man who became an entirely different person when he drank. He knew he had a problem. There were times when he wanted to think he could control his drinking, but it was becoming increasingly hard for him to ignore the reality. Each of his binge episodes was getting worse and the consequences were getting higher.

We checked in at the front desk and Nick went through all the intake assessments they required before he, again, voluntarily signed himself into medical detox. I left him for a day or so until I could get back to visit. The treatment center was a dump, which, believe it or not, is actually a compliment. There were lots of people of all ages from all walks of life coming and going that Sunday afternoon. That's one thing I was beginning to learn through reading and visiting detox and outpatient rehab centers: addiction is a round-the-clock, seven-days-a-week business serving a wildly diverse crowd from all walks of life. Alcohol and drug abuse do not discriminate.

Tom stepped in for me again two nights later and, because visiting hours were almost over, I raced the forty miles to the center in Denton to visit Nick. He was fine, doing what he was told, and abiding by the rules. He thought the place was incredibly boring.

We continued to have, from my perspective, open, honest, two-way conversations. Rob knew I'd flown Nick to Texas and he understood Nick had been overusing alcohol. Rob's comfort zone was pointing fingers and trying to control the situation; thus, I knew it was up to me to take the reins to help Nick turn the situation around. Rob was not going to be helpful; doing so would have required him to examine his own drinking habits and admit he had a major problem, which was out of the question.

My heart had ached tremendously when I listened as Nick cried over the phone, in drunken desperation, about how sad he was, how awful he felt inside. Yet, even when he was really drunk, Nick never alluded to or mentioned committing suicide, just that he felt so sad and alone. Even today, it's hard to acknowledge the depth of despair I felt for this child I loved so much and had tried so hard to give a happy, "normal" life, who felt so empty and found his greatest comfort when he was black-out drunk. Unless you've seen or heard your child in this state of mind, there really is no way to share the depth of the utter despair rolling around in my head during those weeks.

Nick stayed inpatient for the next week and I visited once or twice more. However, the center wasn't very close to our home, even though it was the closest one on our insurance provider's in-network list. And besides Nick, I had four other children for whom to take care. I was an emotional basket case on the inside, but I was determined not to let this show to my family and friends. I had to tell the kids to some degree what was happening in a way that wouldn't scare them. I tried not to dwell on it. The last thing I wanted was them to feel nervous around their brother for any reason. During those months, the only person I really shared my fear and feelings with was my mom. We counseled each other a lot through the whole thing and, for the millionth time in my life, I was so grateful to have her on my side.

Nick's treatment team said the next step for him was a twenty-one-day outpatient program. Initially, he was happy for the change of scenery he'd found in Texas, but it wasn't long before Nick remembered he had left both a girlfriend and a job behind in Wisconsin, and when he thought about committing to another three weeks, he began to waver.

We discussed it thoroughly, I was clear in reminding him to look back on the past three or four months and remember how quickly his life had gotten out of control, reiterating that we weren't in any financial position to keep flying people back and forth across the country every time he fell off the wagon. It was clear we needed to get him in a different direction and if that meant being out of the game of life for three more weeks then that's what he needed to do. Even though he'd worked at Sam's Club for only a few weeks, they told him he could take a leave of absence and wished him well. I have to say, I was impressed they would be willing to take him back given he'd sporadically shown up the first few weeks of employment and was now informing them he was in rehab. It was comforting news for both of us. Though this was before the age of the smartphone, Nick spent a lot of time talking to his girlfriend while he was staying with us. Much to my dismay at the time, their relationship continued in earnest.

Outpatient treatment occurred from 9 a.m. to 1 p.m. For three weeks, I navigated the four younger kids' summer activity schedules between driving Nick to and from Denton twice each day. I was putting an excess of *two hundred miles a day* on the car with all the running around. To say it was a stressful month would be an understatement, but I was committed to doing whatever I could to help Nick. He was involved in a lot of group work and attended AA meetings during the program. He also had plenty of time to spend with his siblings; it had been a while since that happened. His trip to Texas, I believe, was good for all of us. Did I see a dramatic change or shift in Nick after three weeks of outpatient therapy? Not really, but he was more open to talking about his feelings and the family time was good for all of us.

When the program ended there was no choice; it was time to send Nick back to Wisconsin. As I put him on the plane back to Milwaukee and additional house rules at Grandma's (which Nick said he'd fully comply with and totally understood why they were in place), I shook my head and took a deep breath. I was apprehensive because we were just shy of his twenty-first birthday and I hoped and prayed this was the end of the bumps. I spent the last few months waiting for the other shoe to drop and holding my breath when the phone rang. It was very emotionally draining.

Everything went fine for three weeks, and then the phone rang.

WAITING FOR THE OTHER SHOE TO DROP

Nick's twenty-first birthday came and went without incident. I wasn't worried his celebration would center around a big, crazy bar party or anything. Nick's danger with alcohol came from his need to medicate deep-seated feelings of anxiety and depression, not from being a social party king. To mark the occasion, my mom took Nick and his girlfriend out for a nice steak dinner. She wanted to make it a special occasion for him and I was grateful, once again, for all the ways she steps up in my life.

By now it was September 2008, four months after the initial phone call when I found out Nick was battling an alcohol addiction. Nick was working at Sam's Club part time again, occasionally going to AA (although he didn't have a sponsor), and hanging out with his friends in my mom's rec room. He and I talked several times a week; we continued to have good, open dialogue. My mom filled me in on what she saw between our calls. Things seemed to be settling down and I was beginning to feel like I could breathe.

And then, one warm, sunny Sunday evening in late September, just as I was putting dinner on the table, the phone rang. The caller I.D. said "Nick."

"Hi, Nicky Boy!" I answered the phone in a cheerful voice.

"Who is this, please?" a deep, formal voice asked. My heart leapt into my throat.

"My name is Kim Muench," I replied. "I am Nick's mom. Who is this?"

"Ma'am, this is Officer Schmidt with the Pewaukee Police Department," he stated.

Oh Fuck! Oh My God! Oh My God! Oh My God. What happened to my baby?! My mind was racing.

"We have your son at the police station," the officer informed me. "He has been arrested for driving under the influence. He blew a .375 when he was picked up. A driver who noticed he was swerving on the road called the station."

"IS HE OKAY?!" I yelled through the phone.

"At this point, he is passed out and slumped over in a wheelchair."

"Was anyone hurt?" I inquired.

"No, ma'am," the officer assured me.

So many things were going through my head. First and foremost, relief he was alive, then anger because he'd gone on yet another binge, followed by an immediate sense of gratitude for the fact that he didn't injure or kill anyone else.

"Where are you, ma'am, and can you come get him?" the officer continued.

I explained that I lived in Dallas and Nick was currently living with my mother in Brookfield. I refused to have her get involved this time; I couldn't expose her to Nick's destructive behavior any longer. Nick was well-aware of the consequence of any more binge episodes: he'd have to move out. "Officer, here is his dad's phone number; he's local," I told him. "He can deal with this problem today. If you can't get ahold of his dad, he'll just have to sit in jail."

"Ma'am, you do not want him to sit in here," he said. "It's not the place for him at this point."

I wasn't 100% sure what the officer meant by the comment, and I didn't ask.

"Oh, well, I hope you can get hold of his dad then."

And I hung up the phone.

Looking back, I imagine I sounded pretty callous to the officer, but I knew in my heart what I'd done to help Nick over the past several months and, as much as I loved my son and was grateful that he was not splattered all over Highway 16, I was done at the moment. I was so angry he had gone on yet another binge, not to mention my knowledge that he had put countless lives of both strangers and people we knew in danger by driving drunk. The area in which he was pulled over was a central location where many of our family and friends could have been travelling.

After several minutes on the phone, I rejoined my family to eat dinner. Tom knew there must be trouble and all the kids wondered why I was on the phone for so long and hadn't eaten with them. As usual, I made something up and then cleaned up the dinner dishes and got the kids to bed. All the while, at the forefront of my mind was a vivid image of Nick slumped over in a wheelchair at a police station in Wisconsin. I wondered if they'd been able to get in touch with Rob.

By 8:30 p.m., when the kids were down, I called Rob to find out that yes, he'd "picked up [Nick's] drunken ass" from the station and then he and his wife had to "drag his dead-ass weight across the driveway and up the stairs to his bedroom." Rob was clearly angry at Nick and wanted to be sure I knew. We talked for a long time about how Nick living with my mom was not working. We were out of options; Nick would need to return to Rob's house. Part of me felt awful because I knew how much Nick detested even the thought of living with his dad again. He'd made it clear that living with Rob was incredibly difficult. I knew this was the last thing Nick wanted. As far as Rob was concerned, we'd coddled Nick with all these "useless programs" and he needed some sense beaten into him. As I had on many other occasions, I cut off the conversation rather than listen to Rob's hopeless rambling and continuous condescension. In his mind, I was always to blame when there was a problem with Nick, while he had all the answers. There was no working with him to find a way to navigate Nick's alcohol abuse. Seeing how Rob's relationship with Nick was turning out was so sad, mainly because Rob was a chronic alcoholic himself—though he'd never admit it.

Nick and I talked the next day, and, although he was distraught, he knew his grandma's rule and he had absolutely no other place to go. Hindsight being 20/20, I know the weeks he spent under his dad's roof again were some of his darkest moments. Rob ended up taking a house arrest position in the matter. He watched Nick like a hawk, only allowing him to use the car to go to and from work, and he was given very limited contact with his friends. Obviously, Nick needed structure but from what Rob told me, he was treating Nick as if he were in jail. There was absolutely no compassion whatsoever on his dad's part or any willingness to help him by talking to him or trying to find some way to help him communicate his feelings. To be honest, I don't think his dad could help him because he didn't have the mental focus to do so.

Rob and I spoke a couple of times a week about how Nick was doing and what he was up to, and I continued to talk with Nick often as well. Being far away from him was so hard on my heart but I was completely out of ideas on how to help.

During the last week in October, Nick slipped up again. I knew in my heart it was only a matter of time before it was going to happen. Rob found Nick in his car in the driveway passed out drunk. To this day, the details of whether he just sat in his car after work and drank there or if he'd been driving around town drinking are unknown to me. When Rob found Nick, he yanked him out of the car, hitting Nick's head on the door frame and causing a deep gash on the back of his head. Apparently, the wound bled quite a bit and Rob had to hold pressure on it for some time, which greatly annoyed him. He didn't feel the cut warranted a trip to the emergency room, though. The story from that night never made a lot of sense to me, and when I saw the wound on the back of Nick's head shortly thereafter, I was beside myself. The details of the evening will never be fully known to me since I was not present, Nick was passed out drunk, and his dad is no longer living.

When Rob called me to tell me what had happened, I really wanted him to take Nick to the hospital. But Rob said everything was going to be fine. I was completely out of my head, thinking about what was going on in Wisconsin. Nick was always cautious of his dad's temper; he always had been and with good reason. Yet, ironically, because of his drinking, he'd put himself in the most vulnerable position possible. He was literally powerless against his dad's rage and frustration. I couldn't understand why in God's name Nick would have ever allowed himself to be so vulnerable when he was finally physically superior to his father (when sober) for the first time in his life!

Convinced Nick would be dead before the end of the year otherwise, I told Tom I needed to get Nick out of his dad's house and into a long-term rehab program. Tom wasn't happy about another last-minute flight and the cost of rehab admission, but he knew there was no other answer than to allow me to do what needed to be done. Unfortunately, by this time, Nick was no longer covered under our health insurance because he'd dropped out of school, so my next step was to begin searching the internet for inpatient addiction care.

One link led to another and, before I knew it, I was contacting a facility in California. The young man I spoke with there had a similar story to Nick's, had turned his life around, and was now a counselor at the treatment center. The fee for treatment was steep: $40,000 plus airfare to get Nick there, most of which had to be paid upfront. At this point, I knew things were desperate with Nick and I knew Nick understood he needed help, but I was not 100% certain he'd get from Milwaukee to Los Angeles, where a driver from the facility would take him the rest of the way. Even with my parents in Milwaukee to help escort him to the airport, I just didn't know if he'd actually go through with it or get cold feet. Nick had recently left his girlfriend and job to be in Dallas for several weeks of outpatient care, and although he knew he was definitely slipping up again, the thought of stepping so far outside his comfort zone could, indeed, be a huge gamble.

While juggling the daily responsibilities of four kids, school, and extracurricular activities, I was desperately researching

131

how to get Nick the help he needed. There wasn't much time to thoroughly investigate anything and I had no friends or acquaintances to call for advice on this subject. So, I made a verbal commitment to the facility in California and an interviewer called to speak directly with Nick. He asked Nick general questions to get an idea of his level of readiness and explained their treatment program to him.

Determined to get Nick out of this situation and into long-term rehab to save his life, I ended up making arrangements to fly into Milwaukee the morning after Nick's interview to get him on the plane to California. I knew once he agreed to go, there would be an urgency to follow through right away so he didn't change his mind. Once I landed in Milwaukee, I had called Nick's dad to let him know I was in town and wanted to come to his house and sit down with Nick face-to-face. Rob actually sounded relieved I was there, presumably because the events of the past week with Nick had really baffled Rob. My dad picked me up from the airport and took me to my mom's house where the three of us were to discuss the whole financial situation before I surprised Nick at his dad's house. My parents were aware of our financial situation and knew Tom and I didn't have $40k on hand to cough up for the treatment center; they also wanted Nick to get the help he needed. So, I sat down with my parents and did something that gutted me to even think about: I asked for help paying for treatment. Only desperation and love for my child would ever bring me to ask for help this way. Since I left home at eighteen,

I have considered myself to be very strong and independent, but I just couldn't do this without some major financial assistance from my mom and dad. Together, we discussed the details and came up with a plan to finance Nick's treatment. The treatment center needed us to fax a copy of a check for $15,000 in order to secure Nick's spot in the program. The rest would need to be paid shortly after his arrival. While Dad took care of that detail, I borrowed Mom's car and went out to Rob's house to confront our son.

THE ROCKY ROAD TO REHAB

Twenty minutes later, I quietly knocked on Rob's front door. I hadn't seen Rob in about three years; when he appeared in the doorway, I was shocked at his appearance. Both his face and body–especially his midsection–were really bloated, and his eyes were no longer white but yellow. I thought to myself, *My God, he will never make it to forty-five. This is such a shame.* Rob let me in and then he yelled up the stairs for Nick. As Nick appeared and came down the stairs, he was clearly surprised to see me.

"Nick, I love you," I told my son. "God has sent me here today for one of two reasons: either to take you to rehab or to say goodbye to you because you won't live much longer."

I was crying hard as Nick stood directly in front of me. We hugged.

"Mom, I can't go to that facility," Nick told me in a stern voice. "I've spent some time investigating it, and I think it's a coverup for a cult."

"WHAT?!" I exclaimed.

He repeated himself.

"No, that's not true," I insisted. "I've spoken at length with this place and it sounds like just what you need."

"Mom, come up to my room and I'll show you."

We went upstairs and Rob left us alone. Nick pulled up a news story on the internet, which appeared to be an in-depth report on the treatment center I'd chosen. Sure enough, the news report made it appear to the outside world like this facility operated to help with addiction, yet behind the scenes it was a religious cult aligned with the Church of Scientology.

Oh My God! Oh My God!

My brain was screaming, knowing my dad had just faxed a $15,000 check to these people! Trying not to panic, I prayed they would do the right thing and not cash the check until they heard from me. My family didn't have this kind of money to lose. My next thought was *Holy shit, here I am in Milwaukee, and I have absolutely no plan for what comes next.*

Suddenly, Rob stuck his head in the room and reminded Nick he had to get to work. I knew we needed more time to discuss things and come up with an alternate plan, so I told Rob I'd drop Nick at work. Rob was satisfied with that plan, so the two of us left. The second we pulled away from the house, I turned to Nick.

"You know you aren't going to work today, right?" I asked.

"Yes," he said. "But I do want to stop and say goodbye."

I didn't trust the situation at all, so when we got to Sam's Club I went in with Nick and we spoke to his manager together. She was very supportive, told me how well Nick was doing there, and said he was welcome to come back when he was in better mental health. We thanked her and got back in the car.

Back at my mom's house, the three of us talked about what needed to happen next. I felt strongly that Nick needed to go far away for inpatient rehabilitation rather than in-state where it would be easier to walk away or to have his dad, his girlfriend, and other friends visit him. He needed to focus on himself. Nick agreed. He was willing to get help and wanted to be able to move out of his dad's house.

Mom's computer wasn't working at the moment, so Nick and I drove to the local library and spent the afternoon researching addiction facilities specifically for young adults. Florida, Arkansas, and Minnesota all had programs that looked interesting but it was all so overwhelming, confusing, and costly. Then La Hacienda in Hunt, Texas popped up. An avid Dr. Phil fan at the time, I remembered him sending people from his show there for treatment. After gathering a bunch of phone numbers, we returned to Mom's house where the three of us talked about what Nick and I found.

"Kim, the facility in Texas you mentioned might be a good place. It's in your state, which might allow you to visit during his stay even though it's still six hours away."

True. So, I called La Hacienda and spoke with an intake counselor for a long time, learning about their program, the costs, the family week required for us to attend. I felt very comfortable with the program and the man with whom I spoke. Admittedly, I was very cautious because of the previous fiasco. Fortunately, the treatment center in California never cashed the check. They swore to me they were not a religious cult masquerading as an addiction recovery facility. But it didn't matter—I'd moved on, though I still wept with relief for having their cooperation.

It was late Saturday afternoon and I knew Rob would be expecting Nick to come home from work. I called Rob and told him what we'd actually been doing since we left his house. Of course, he was angry at me for lying to him, but I stuck to my guns, reminding him how things had gone the past few weeks and asking him what other options he thought we might have. I arranged for Nick to come by shortly to pick up his belongings because he would be leaving for Texas Monday morning with me. The plan was for me to fly with Nick to San Antonio, drive to the facility to drop him off, then fly back to Dallas. Lots of last-minute airfares only added to the overall expense, but it was the only way I felt comfortable he'd see it through. I wanted to be with Nick, not only to be sure he got there, but also to ensure that he knew he had my full love, support, and encouragement.

Before we went back to Rob's that night, I told Nick to get absolutely everything he wanted while we were there. Rob was still a bit surly and edgy about the whole thing, still pissed I'd lied to him about getting Nick to work. Rob liked to think he was in charge and every good idea was his own. It wasn't worth fighting or arguing with him. The greater good would be served when Nick was out of this picture. In the meantime, he and I needed to work together to get his personal belongings out of his dad's house. I told him to take as long as he needed to pack and I would hang out with his dad.

For about an hour, Nick went up and down the stairs, organizing and packing his stuff, hauling his things out to his car while I listened to his dad rant about everything from the weather to the condition of his knees. While Rob rambled as we sat in his living room, I became completely amazed at how he'd deteriorated over the past few years. My heart hurt for him. Rob's wife of many years sat by his side and barely said a word unless it was to agree with something Rob said. Even though they'd been married for more than a decade and she'd been a regular part of Nick's life, she and I never exchanged more than pleasantries. It wasn't that I had anything against her; I just didn't have any idea how she felt about me. And I got the feeling Rob didn't want us to talk. Based on Nick's sharing over the years, I believe Rob's wife endured a great deal of physical, mental, and emotional abuse during their marriage. I have no direct proof, just my own experience with Rob when I dated him, but I can't imagine the wife of a career alcoholic would escape unscathed.

Once Nick was finally ready, he hugged his dad and stepmom,

telling them he loved them and would be in touch soon. I vividly remember mentally taking a picture of the scene, wondering if it would be the last Nick would ever see or touch his dad. Something in me confirmed that would be the case. Nick and I got into our respective cars and left. We stopped up the block and I rolled down my window.

"We did it!" I yelled. "Let's go out for pizza!"

We stopped at our favorite pizza place and had a nice dinner together. Nick and I talked about the change in scenery this would give him, the new start he wanted. Of course, he was concerned about leaving his girlfriend again but knew he needed more help to change direction than he'd previously had. I truly felt like Nick finally understood the gravity of his current situation and really wanted to change his fully-admitted addiction to abusing alcohol as a way to cope with daily stress and anxiety levels. Overall, it was a great dinner.

Afterward, Nick and I drove back to my mom's house and he asked if his girlfriend could come over. When she arrived, the two of them disappeared to the rec room to watch a movie while mom and I talked and flipped television stations in her family room. The three of us went to bed early that night with a feeling all the right events were falling into place; concrete help was on the horizon.

Mom and I got up early the next morning and went to church. Dad was at mass and came over to the house afterward for coffee and to talk with Nick. Surprisingly, Nick was already up for the day at 10 a.m. We were happy to see he was in a good mood as the four of us sat together and discussed Nick's sobriety and his future. My dad started lecturing Nick about how this really needed to be a new start for him and how it was expensive, but we all loved him and wanted him to turn things around. Toward the end of the conversation, Nick asked if he could go say goodbye to a friend, pick up some cigarettes, and do some last-minute banking before leaving town early the next morning. I thought nothing of this and said he could go. I knew he was on- board with going to rehab. Nick understood we had a flight to San Antonio booked for very early the next day and he was all ready to go.

Nick ran his errands, Dad left, and I considered how I was going to approach Rob for some money–anything he could afford–to help the cost involved for inpatient treatment at La Hacienda. The total bill for Nick's six-week stay would be $36,000—half due on arrival, the other half due ten days into his treatment. Tom and I could only afford to put in $5,000 (plus all the airfare); my dad said he'd give us $4,000, which still left a large chunk to be paid. My grandpa had passed away earlier that year, and mom had enough inheritance to pay the rest, but I didn't want her to use so much of her money. I hated the idea of groveling for money from Rob, but I was trapped in a corner and my kid needed serious help. Thus, I was hellbent and on a mission; my pride took a back seat to everything else. I was willing to eat a hefty helping of humble pie, if necessary.

So, I called Rob and asked to see him. We met, once again, in his living room; I explained the financial situation to him and asked for his help. Rob flat-out told me he was knee-deep in debt and couldn't help me. I was so desperate I even asked him to ask his mom for some money (since he'd always been so forthcoming about how wealthy she was). Rob told me he'd never let his mom know about Nick's troubles with alcohol because if she knew it would kill her. So, I walked away with nothing. Not exactly surprising, but I had been optimistic.

Back at Mom's, I briefly wondered where Nick was but wasn't too concerned. A few minutes later, he walked into the kitchen with a piece of equipment he'd picked up to fix my mom's computer before leaving town. Helping her get her computer working again was something he'd been promising he'd do for a while. Nick went upstairs to work on the computer, but five minutes later he came back down to the kitchen where Mom and I were talking.

"I just can't get the piece to work," he announced.

We both looked up.

"Oh well," my mom replied. "I've lived without it this long. Don't worry about it."

Nick didn't really respond. He then stepped through the back door onto her patio and lit a cigarette. Something immediately struck both Mom and I. We looked at one another.

"Oh my God," I said. "I think he's been drinking."

My heart stopped. Without saying a word, Mom went outside to sit with him while I checked his car and room. Sure enough, I found a nearly empty, full-size bottle of vodka tucked into his trusty backpack in the trunk of his car. *Fuck!* My mind was racing, trying to figure out what to do next. We had airline tickets booked for early the next morning. *My kid's gotta get to rehab but right now he's drunk and I know from being on the phone with him during these binges his behavior will get worse and will go on for hours.* It was clear Nick had been drinking; there was quite a bit gone from the bottle. *Okay. Slow down, breathe, keep it together, and don't panic.* I said this to myself over and over as if saying it enough times might actually make me believe it.

Quickly, I checked the rest of the car, his room, and then dumped out what I'd found in Mom's kitchen sink. Mom called me to join them on the patio. On my way out the door, she passed me coming in and I told her I'd pretty much searched everything, tossed the booze I'd found, and taken his keys. I was stupid enough to think maybe I'd redirected the situation in that moment and we could salvage the original plan of action. Since I had only found one bottle, it was tough to know if he'd drank a bottle before he got home and how much alcohol was in his system now. I was so pissed at myself for being duped by him and that he'd had the nerve to deceive my mom and me! *What in God's name was he thinking?!* I went outside and sat down next to him. I'll admit, I was scared.

Although I was fully ready to take my son to rehab and had heard him babble on and on incessantly on the phone while drunk, I'd never actually *seen* him drunk. In my mind, I just kept asking God for help and clarity on what to do, over and over.

I asked Nick if he'd been drinking. At first, he tried to deny it, but his slurred speech, droopy head, and the way his body draped across a lounge chair that Sunday afternoon didn't support his answer. As I tried to keep him talking while simultaneously praying and figuring out what to do next, Nick began to get emotional. Tears started falling down his cheeks; he said he wanted to share some things with me but needed to drink more before he could. He stood up and tried to go toward his car and look for his bottle. I followed him, trying to dissuade him.

When he discovered it wasn't in the backpack in his trunk, Nick immediately got angry because he knew we'd taken his vodka. Both mom and I tried to talk with him, calmly, about sleeping it off because we had a plane to catch early in the morning. Nick quickly got belligerent and threw my mom into the wall in her laundry room, sending a set of decorative dishes that were hanging on the wall crashing to the floor. Exchanging wide-eyed looks of desperate astonishment, Mom and I knew things were getting out of hand, fast. It was clear we needed help.

In an effort to pacify him until I could get someone who could help, I told Nick if he would calm down and watch TV with Grandma for a few minutes, I'd run across the street to the grocery store and get one bottle of whatever he wanted so he could talk to me about his feelings. It took a few minutes to convince him; he wanted to come with me, but I didn't back down, so he finally calmed down enough to relent.

I got into the car, pulled out of the driveway and, once out of sight, called 911. Waiting in a nearby parking lot, I calmly explained the situation to the dispatcher and she sent two squad cars. I gave the officers a high-level summary of the previous few months with Nick and the current situation Mom and I were in. I shared that we had airline tickets to San Antonio booked for the next day – Monday – where a ride would take us to the rehab facility we had chosen. The two officers offered to come and talk with Nick but said there was not much else they could do for me. Since that was better than nothing, I agreed.

We all pulled into the driveway together and walked into mom's living room where she and Nick were watching television. My mom's expression let me know she was surprised to see the police officers, then turned to relief that someone was there to help. Nick stood up, angry at first, but then became highly compliant with the officers. Nick, the two officers, and I sat down together at the kitchen table and the officers asked Nick some basic questions. One of them asked if she could run a breathalyzer on him to check his BAC. He agreed, telling the officers he wasn't even close to drunk. He blew a 0.18 (the legal limit in Wisconsin is 0.08). Nick was wide awake, alert, not slurring, but not making much sense either.

The officers stayed for about an hour longer, chatting with Nick about different things, reminding him he'd made a commitment to go to rehab and how much his mom and grandma loved him, so it was important to follow through and be a man about going ahead with the plan to get on the plane the next morning. And, they reiterated, additional alcohol would not be part of that plan. The officers' shift was ending and they needed to leave. Nick was much calmer than he'd been before they arrived. Mom stayed with Nick while I walked the officers outside. They wished me well and said there was nothing more they could do unless he got behind the wheel of a car or became violent. I thanked them profusely for their time and assistance. We had agreed, before they left, to watch a movie and have dinner. So, when I came back inside, Nick and I sat down to watch TV while mom began making dinner. Less than two minutes later, Nick stood up and said he was going outside for a cigarette. I urged him to wait until the movie was over, or to let me go outside with him, but was unsuccessful. He finally just turned and walked straight out the door.

Knowing he would walk across the very busy, six-lane divided highway to the grocery store to steal alcohol (he had no wallet on him), I quickly looked up the grocery store's number. I called and asked for the manager. Very calmly, I told him my son would be walking into the store within the next five minutes. I described Nick's physical features as well as the clothes he was wearing. I said he'd make a beeline for the liquor department and he was already legally drunk. The manager told me he'd be on the lookout for him. I then went outside, stood at the end of Mom's driveway, and aggressively prayed while simultaneously listening for the squeal of tires as he staggered into busy traffic. I told myself it was better if he was arrested for stealing; at least he'd be safe in jail for the night. I kept waiting to hear sirens but heard nothing except cars rushing by.

After twenty minutes or so, I gave up and went back into the house. Mom and I were talking, trying to process everything that had gone on during the past few hours and agree on what we should do next when, suddenly, Nick walked in the door. He was clearly staggering and nearly unconscious. I helped him over to a bar stool at the kitchen counter and told him dinner was almost ready. *Why the hell was I even pretending dinner was going to be an option?* Nick's head slumped onto the countertop. I said his name and he looked up and began to move his arm in a strange and repetitive way. He was talking gibberish and making no sense. Nick had obviously had more alcohol—or something else. He then broke out into a profuse sweat; he was immediately soaked. I'd never seen anything like it! Once again, Mom and I looked at each other, both scared about what was happening. Frantically, I picked up the phone and called 911 for the second time that day. Within five minutes of relaying Nick's condition to the dispatcher, several first response vehicles were outside the house.

Thank God for police officers, firefighters, and paramedics because they came in and took over. Mom and I both felt relieved things were at least a little under control. Not that we thought everything would necessarily be okay, but there was positive forward motion with the emergency team in her house. I watched the paramedics lay my son on the kitchen floor, trying to get information from him as they began to work on him. All that kept going through my head were the words I'd said to him the previous day when I appeared at this dad's house (*was that only the day before?!*). I told Nick I was standing before him for one of two reasons: to take him to rehab or to say goodbye to him because he wouldn't live much longer the way things were going. It struck me hard, as I watched the scene unfolding in front of me; I didn't know which way it was going to go.

They managed to get Nick stabilized; he was experiencing alcohol-induced seizures. I grabbed Nick's phone as the paramedics loaded him into the ambulance. Mom and I followed them to the local emergency room. Nick had hidden an additional bottle of whiskey, which we later found thrown in a bush outside Mom's house. He'd only been gone about thirty minutes. Obviously, the store manager never saw him come into the store.

When we arrived at the hospital, I scrolled through the contact list on Nick's phone. I called his girlfriend and his former roommate, Mark. Nick had mentioned he'd seen Mark earlier in the day and I was hoping he could help me piece together whether there was anything else Nick might have in his system or if Nick had already been drinking when Mark saw him. Mark said Nick was fine when he saw him and Mark had not given him any kind of drugs while they were together. For some reason, I believed him.

Shortly after I made the calls, Mark showed up at the hospital with Nick's girlfriend and Hambo, another friend of Nick's who I'd never met. I told the three of them what had gone on during the afternoon. We were called into the room to see Nick a few minutes later. Nurses and doctors shuffled in and out of the room; Nick lay on the bed, conscious and rambling. For the next two hours, we all took shifts in the room with him. When Nick's girlfriend was in the room with him, he seemed to get very upset and verbal; thank goodness he was immobilized due to his condition. Two police officers were stationed outside his door to ensure things remained civilized.

Sitting with Nick's friends was really eye-opening for me. I learned a lot more about my son from a totally different perspective. There was so much I didn't know about what had been happening in his life since we'd moved to Dallas. At times, my jaw dropped in astonishment that my son, who I thought I knew well, was really someone who I knew nothing about at all. At one point during the evening while I was in the waiting room, Nick's friend Hambo, who was a very big, teddy-bear kind of guy, told me he'd be happy to help in any way he could. Though I'd never heard of him before, he and Nick had apparently spent a lot of time together. I could tell his offer came straight from his heart. The whole day had been over-the-top—physically, mentally, emotionally.

The nurse informed me they would keep Nick overnight for observation and then the police would escort him to the county detention facility for a mandatory twenty-four-hour stay. It didn't matter if we had plane tickets for the next morning, or that Nick had a bed waiting for him at La Hacienda. He had to be detained. Since there wasn't much left to do at the hospital, we said goodbye to Nick. Mom and I went home. It was after 10 p.m., neither of us had eaten, and we both were totally drained. I also had to cancel the airline tickets and let La Hacienda know we wouldn't be arriving the next day.

Deciding to take Hambo up on his offer of help, I asked him to fly along with Nick and me as insurance to get him to the treatment center. Hambo would be with Nick if he needed to use the bathroom, he could help me entertain Nick, and, if necessary, step in as the strong physical presence I might need along the way. At this point, I wasn't taking any chances at all. Hambo was very happy for a free ride to and from Dallas to be Nick's bodyguard.

I didn't visit Nick in the county detention facility until it was time to go to the airport on Tuesday. As grateful as I was that he ended up being physically okay, I was still angry and hurt he'd gone for one last hurrah while knowing we had everything in order to leave. It was clear I still had a lot to learn about addiction.

Mom drove us to the airport; we didn't stop for anything, not for a bathroom break, not for a cigarette, nothing. Nick, Hambo, and I flew to San Antonio to meet up with a driver from La Hacienda who took us the additional seventy-five miles to the treatment facility. There were so many times during our journey when I was happy that I'd paid for Hambo to ride along. Though Nick was agreeable and ready to seek long-term, inpatient help, he wrestled with cold feet at leaving his girlfriend and there were a few times Hambo definitely helped smooth things over in a way I couldn't. He made Nick laugh with stories of things they'd done together (granted, those stories involved many party nights from previous years) and other topics young-adult guys share.

Tuesday was a long day; we finally arrived at La Hacienda just before 10 p.m. When we got there, I gave the intake counselor a large check and kissed my son goodbye. I told Nick I loved him and I would talk to him soon. Hambo and I rode quietly back to the airport with the La Hacienda driver. Unfortunately, I'd just missed the last flight of the night to Dallas. Hambo had a flight back to Milwaukee at six the next morning, so he and I found a quiet corner in the airport and tried to while away the next six hours before our respective flights departed.

The airport was frigid and the only noise was the incessant

droning of the television repeatedly announcing our new president: Barack Obama. The perfect end to an unbelievable week was resurrecting my dirty laundry out of my carry-on bag so I could lay it on the dirty carpet and try to cover myself against the chill of the air conditioning. Poor Hambo had worn shorts and a t-shirt and didn't think to bring anything along with him, so he lay right on the hard floor (snoring like a madman because he had a bad cold). Neither of us had planned for this when we left Milwaukee. Looking back, it would have been smarter to find a bench outside the airport and sleep under the stars in the warm, humid, November San Antonio night.

I've had some long nights as a mother, but that one took the cake!

LESSONS LEARNED

I was naïve to believe once I delivered Nick into an inpatient treatment program everything would be fine and, although we'd definitely remember all we'd been through, life would go back to "normal." Addiction, whether it's to alcohol, drugs, shopping, sex, gambling, or whatever, is a disease. There are ups and downs and we experienced our share of both with Nick for some time after his stay at La Hacienda.

Three weeks into Nick's treatment, Tom, Allen-Michael, and I made the six-hour drive from Dallas to Hunt, TX to attend their Family Program. We brought Allen-Michael along because Tom and I felt he, at age fifteen, would benefit from the education we'd receive about addiction, and we also felt he was mature enough to understand more about what was going on with his older brother. Allen-Michael has since told us what an impactful experience the family program was to his life.

Nick did not invite his dad to come down from Wisconsin for the family program because he didn't feel ready to deal with their relationship. Truth be told, I don't know if at the time his dad would have been physically well enough to fly. During his recovery, I learned about several things Nick kept from me for many years out of the fierce loyalty he had to Rob. One of the things I had to reconcile with was even though I'd managed to get myself out of an abusive situation, I didn't get my child out of it, and, in fact, may have inadvertently made things much worse for him because his dad's rage needed new direction since I was no longer in the picture.

While attending the four-day program, we listened to a lot of lectures, journaled, and participated in teamwork exercises both within our family as well as in combination with other families who were attending the session. Through these events, we all learned a great deal about the disease of addiction, our family, and ourselves.

A few weeks later, at the end of his inpatient treatment, Nick decided to go into sober living in Austin. He continued to struggle with a lot of anxiety, and it got the better of him shortly after he left treatment. Although he'd learned some solid coping skills through La Hacienda, he fell back to the one he'd been using since age fifteen, drinking alcohol to dull his intense feelings. This happened to him a handful of times over the next few months, but he continued to get back up each time with more resolve than before. As I write this today, I am so blessed to tell you Nick celebrated a decade of sobriety on May 20, 2020. He is happily married and works full-time in information technology.

Rob passed away in February 2010 at the age of forty-two, a direct result of physical and mental complications from his years of alcohol abuse. It turns out I was right about his and Nick's hug in the driveway being the very last moment he and

Nick would ever share. Rob called Nick on occasion during the years between Nick's leaving for treatment and Rob's untimely death, but Nick rarely spoke with him because he was trying so hard to stay sober, and the sound of his dad's voice rocked him to the core. I know Nick wishes things had turned out differently, I do as well. I hope and believe Rob was able to find some peace in death; his time on Earth was punctuated with misery he often took out on others.

Because Nick didn't regularly keep in contact with him, Rob's death was a surprise to him and it gutted his emotional state and sobriety. Nick struggled and binged a great deal for three months after he attended the funeral. He ended up in jail not once but twice. These were some of the most difficult moments I faced as his mom. Of course, on some level, I actually felt Nick was in a safe place when in jail. The hardest thing I have ever done as a mom was not bail him out. As difficult and uncomfortable as I knew he was behind bars, I would not, and will not, ever help him duck the consequences of his action — even if he was black-out drunk at the time and didn't remember what happened. Staying detached when your child is going through something really big is brutal, and one of the most growth-inducing experiences for a parent.

When I think back on Nick's teen years, I know I was in denial while he was in high school, thinking he didn't drink. Aside from raising Nick, I had four children and a marriage I was working on. I'm not making excuses for what I missed or what I denied. I just don't know if I would have been able to stop all of the destructive events from happening even if I had been more aware or less in denial.

I believe we are largely powerless as parents over so many things and can't possibly protect our kids from some of life's challenges, as much as we'd like to shield them from any unhappy circumstances. These are their life lessons to learn. In reflecting on my own life, I know my personal challenges have provided opportunities not only to become stronger but also more compassionate, empathetic, resilient, and tolerant.

As kids grow into their uncertain and often tumultuous adolescence, we parents need to adjust the way we relate to them, gradually shifting from teaching **over** them into consulting **with** them. Our job is to become their guides, to listen openly, to set clear and firm boundaries in areas of their safety, and to love them unconditionally for who they are, not who we need or want them to be.

Kids will make mistakes and unhealthy choices at times. We did, too. They aren't given to us to meet, exceed, or live out our expectations; they are brought into the world **through** us to live out the journey intended *for them*. As their Mom or Dad, we are blessed to be a part of the process and, if we choose to do so, can grow ourselves up as we raise our children.

I am so grateful and inspired by the man Nick has become. He has been able to climb out of a very dark hole and continues to work on his life in positive ways. I will always love, support, and encourage him, while never willingly enabling self-destructive behavior (and this carries over to all of the kids who have come through me). I am able to do this knowing I live by faith, calmness, courage, patience, and grace. These characteristics can help each of us achieve our highest potential during our lifetimes.

Becoming Me While Raising You

THE TRUE BELIEFS THAT REFLECT WHO I AM

Experiencing addiction through Nick's struggle was the catalyst I needed to begin an intentional chapter of personal growth, the result of which was my becoming aware about the limiting beliefs that shaped my life. This awareness was cultivated by reading books, like this one, about other people's experiences with self-change. One that sticks out in my head is Bronnie Ware's *The Top Five Regrets of the Dying*. It also came from teachers like Dr. Brené Brown and thought-leaders such as Neale Donald Walsch, whose books I have devoured since seeing him speak at a conference in 2015.

The unconscious belief system I had been working from most of my adult life kept me from trusting my intuition or using my voice. Instead, I made decisions based more on what others wanted or needed me to be for them rather than being true to myself. Each time I did so I abandoned myself. This is so easy for women to do since, as a culture, we are taught to put everyone else's needs above our own, especially when it comes to motherhood.

Designing new beliefs to better serve the relationship I have with myself and with others didn't happen overnight but through continuous self-examination. Over time, I asked tough questions and uncovered beliefs about myself in order to create new ones that felt more truthful; my limiting beliefs were born randomly in bits and pieces over several years, as a result of what other people projected onto me. It's an evolution and I will always be working on my truth.

When Nick left treatment and started sober living, I decided I wanted to go back to college. After walking through addiction alongside him, I felt called to work with teens struggling with substance abuse. As part of my bachelor's degree in psychology, which also contributed to my emotional growth, I intentionally took all the classes I could related to substance abuse treatment. After passing the Texas State LCDC Exam and getting 1,000 hours into my 4,000 internship requirements, I realized helping teens who didn't think they had a substance use problem was not what I wanted to do. *Helping their parents* was the part of my job I loved best, and that's where I wanted to focus my efforts.

During these years I began to pay closer attention to my life, questioning the choices I made about what I welcomed into my days through the television programming I watched, books I read, music I listened to, the people I associated with, and how I spent my free time.

For example, when I turned the dial on the radio station as I connected the dots between Mia singing along with Rihanna and knowing she was potentially internalizing those lyrics in the back of the minivan, once I knew, I couldn't *not know*. Did I want to live my life unconsciously, going through the motions, or did I want to consciously choose my thoughts, words, actions, and beliefs? My desire was clear to me: I no longer wanted to live by default.

Just because I *knew* these things didn't mean I immediately had the courage to take action. First, I merely observed my life, a practice that continues today. In fact, one of the areas I am (finally) now working on is becoming more mindful of and intentional with what I am eating and drinking each day. After more than three decades, my habit of a glass of white wine at night before bed is starting to weigh on me (literally). This doesn't mean I've stopped having the glass of wine altogether, but it's a first step. I also pay attention to what I'm thinking and the words coming out of my mouth: asking myself regularly if what I am thinking, saying, and doing aligns with who I want to be in the world. *Is this who I want to be?* I ask myself. *Do I want to have these thoughts, these feelings, say these things, do these things?* While we don't control much of what goes on around us, we do control who we are in any given situation and how we decide to respond to our life experiences.

I AM WORTH LISTENING TO

I wrote the first iteration of this book in 2011 under the title *My Mother's Footprints: A Story of Faith, Calm, Courage, Patience, and Grace*. A friend of mine's then-husband was a printer and connected me with a small Colorado company that, for a reasonable price, was able to take my story from a Word doc to an actual book. I decided to invest in 500 copies of my book and then sold [some of] them through my very first website (mymothersfootprints.com, of course). I had asked Nick to design a website for me because I enjoyed writing the book so much that I wanted to continue the activity by occasionally creating blog posts. In all honesty, I probably gave more of the books away than I actually sold but I shared them with intention to people I felt would benefit from my experience of parenting through adolescent addiction.

Publishing the book, having the first few people read it, and their positive feedback gave me the courage to ask a local nonprofit drug education support group for the opportunity to speak at one of their meetings. While the thought of doing this filled me with dread because I absolutely hated the idea of talking in front of people, I believed my experience as the mother of an alcoholic in recovery was worth hearing. There is not enough truth in the world and even fewer people willing to share their authentic experience, so I was determined — as difficult and uncomfortable as it was — to be one of the people transparent enough to inspire others to do so.

Over the years, and in small steps, I've been given the opportunity to speak in front of many groups of all sizes. I've spoken in school auditoriums, healthcare settings, and on dozens of national and international podcasts. Since the beginning of the pandemic, I've even been interviewed about conscious parenting a handful of times on our local ABC affiliate in Dallas!

People ask me to tell them exactly how I've done this work and I readily share that sometimes creating a new belief about yourself is as easy as deciding one day what you currently operate from isn't serving you and it's time to move on. Yes, it's just that simple... yet, not that easy. It has never been 100% easy to get up in front of groups of people to talk about my parenting experience and passion for helping other people develop happier, healthier relationships with their kids by parenting WITH rather than over them. But I am fueled to show up and do hard things by my drive to become a conduit for the changes I see need to be made in the way we parent kids!

Speaking in public is one level of going from feeling I'm not worthy of being heard to knowing what I have to say is worth hearing. Working on this in the relationships closest to my heart is another.

When my dad finished reading the first iteration, he called me and, through tears, told me how much he'd enjoyed the story. He also told me how much he'd learned about my side of being pregnant at eighteen. He felt I could have been so much more revengeful about the part he played having to grow up so quickly when becoming a mom for the first time. I told him then, and I'd do the same now, writing this book is not about getting revenge on anyone. Sharing my story is meant to be a channel for truth, one I have grown from and hope to impact others' journeys with as well. The older my dad gets, the more open-minded he's become: it's a good thing.

THE GREATEST SOURCE OF LOVE
AND APPROVAL COMES FROM ME

I used to feel like I had to be a "good girl" in order to be loved and gain approval from others. But over the years I have learned to pursue my passions with input from others rather than allowing others to dictate my actions. After much soul searching (and reading Bronnie Ware's book mentioned earlier) I recently decided to leave my job and go full-time into parent coaching, writing, and speaking on the topic of conscious parenting. Making this leap was serious and significant to my family, especially during the pandemic; not only was my job the only steady income we had between 2018-2020, it also covered our family's health insurance. Saying goodbye to that security was no small decision and it did not come with Tom's support. Nonetheless my gut consistently told me it was time for me to put all of my effort into my passion for helping families.

It's easy to do something when you've got the support of those you love; it's considerably harder when they don't see what you see in your passion and instead feel you need to "do the right thing," which, in this case, was to be responsible for keeping the family afloat financially. Because my husband had done that for years himself, he wasn't happy with my desire to opt out of what he felt was my obligation to the family now.

An important sidenote: Tom left his job in corporate America after 30 years in advertising sales. He chose, with my full support, to open a brick-and-mortar travel franchise—it actually has the word *cruise* in the name. Tom's passion for helping others plan forever-memories with their loved ones through vacations led him to take that big step in mid-2017. I was proud of him for making this leap of faith and supported his decision by getting a part-time job to cover our health insurance while trying to continue to build my coaching business.

From January 2018 to December 2020 I learned, worked, and did well at my job while juggling entrepreneurship. Anyone building a business knows this is tough. One of the main messages I share with parents is to practice taking good care of themselves so they can be both physically present and emotionally attuned to their teenager. These kids need us! Although I loved my job and had a wonderful boss who was super supportive of my part-time coaching business, I struggled with my schedule and the day-to-day demands of my work, business, and family life. On one hand, I was preaching what I felt was a very important message to others, but, on the other hand, I was not living out that message with my own teens, Maddux and Mia. So many things fell through the cracks, and often during those three years I felt like I was half-assing everything. I attempted to quit once in late 2019 but then found out I needed a hysterectomy, and I needed our health insurance to cover so this lengthened my stay. I continued the path until I finally found, and used, my voice in July 2020 when I told Tom I just could not do it any longer.

Obviously, 2020 had a major impact on his second full year in the travel business. Things were just beginning to take root and grow. He'd spent 2018-2019 focused on building a team of consultants, raising awareness locally for the brand and making solid business connections. So, when the pandemic shutdown hit in early 2020, it meant cruises for the entire year and well into 2021 were cancelled. As of this writing, we are just beginning to get news of when ships will sail out of American ports again. By the way, in case you don't know, cruise lines don't pay commissions until they actually sail. That's a long time without any income and to be living off of savings.

I haven't regretted my decision to stop being what others needed me to be and listen to my intuition about the life I'm living. Two entrepreneurs in the house during a pandemic is not easy. It takes a lot of faith to believe you can pursue your dreams of helping others by doing what you love, while holding space that you'll keep a roof over your head and food in your family's mouths!

I CAN TRUST MY INTUITION

One of the hardest lessons we can learn as a parent, speaking both personally and professionally, is how little control we have over the choices and paths our kids' lives take. We often start out very much in control of when they eat, drink, sleep (sort of), and we literally have to carry them or they wouldn't go anywhere. Then, as they start to walk and talk, their brains begin to process more and their thinking separates from our ability to fully influence it, which is as it should be. We begin to understand we don't have control of everything. We have to trust both ourselves and our kids that all of us will be able to handle the bumps that inevitably come with growing up. If we don't, our anxiety will lead us to disconnect from ourselves and our children.

The older our kids get, the less control we have, though we delude ourselves into thinking we still have a fair amount of say over their lives. One day, though, often when we drop them off at college (or they graduate from high school and move into their next chapter), we realize we really have no control at all. Sure, we can threaten them with taking away their car or cell phone, or pulling them out of college if they don't meet our academic/behavior expectations, but that kind of relationship with a young adult will lead to little or no quality connection with them pretty fast. There comes a point when we need to let go and allow the chips to fall where they may as the modeling we've done for so many years takes its hold.

For example, with Nick's addiction to alcohol, I had to acknowledge I played a role in it, partly because I spent a lot of time avoiding his dad after we broke up. Although Nick and I had [what I felt was] good communication during his teen years, my lack of engagement with his dad meant I didn't know how much his dad was actually drinking and how it affected his relationship with Nick. Those months of Nick's downward spiral were some of the most agonizing of my life. Knowing your child is drinking copious amounts of alcohol to drown his sadness, anxiety, depression, and OCD symptoms to the point of blacking out filled me with sorrow, guilt, and a deep sense of helplessness at times. I've not been one to pray often; I would describe myself as inconsistently religious up until about five years ago, and now I choose to be fully spiritual. However, there are times when prayer seems like the only thing you can do. There were many moments during 2008-2010 when I begged God to let Nick live in peace, not for my sake, but for his own.

Those years and my experience with Nick allowed me to understand I needed, for my own sanity, to embrace detaching from the outcome for all the kids I am parenting. We do not know why our children have come into the world through us; we can only love, support, and encourage them where they are in their life's journey. It's a simultaneously liberating and frightening revelation. I have decided to focus on the former.

With each of the kids, trusting them and myself have shown up in different ways. Allen-Michael is currently in his third year of seminary, studying to become a Catholic priest. Allen-Michael is choosing the one path where he will never be able to experience the joy of marriage and parenthood. So often, throughout his twenty-seven years, I've thought he would make a wonderful husband and father. His calm, deep-thinking nature, and desire to serve others shape his character; his dedication and hard-work ethic are essential qualities to both of those life vocations. He was, and still is, a terrific brother to the other kids by continuing to engage with them and care about their lives, no matter how busy he is and no matter how awkward it is to connect with his teenage siblings. Allen-Michael feels deeply called to dedicate his life to the teaching and sharing of the Catholic faith. I no longer practice Catholicism and I grieved his decision, simply because I knew he wouldn't be a husband or dad. After much reflection, I fully accepted and embraced his journey. He and I have wonderful deep discussions and I very much enjoy the man he's become.

Detaching from the outcome and trusting both myself and the universe sometimes involves grief. With Allen-Michael, this meant acknowledging and grieving for what will never be. We are not bad parents if we have ideas about what our kids will be or what we want for them. It's when we try to impose our will on their lives that it becomes detrimental to their evolution. We don't know their path best. They do, and what they have to experience to get there is often out of our control.

Where I will need to become more understanding and trusting of my intuition and detaching from the outcome in my marriage and with the other three kids remains to be seen. Sure, there have been small examples, like watching Maddux put down his bō staff after years of practice and tournament triumphs, or Mia decide to give up her acting career at the tender age of six when (to me) she beamed like a star on the stage. However, this is a hard but necessary part of parenthood: allowing our children to grow into who *they're* meant to be, and not who we want them to be. This is how we show them how to trust themselves as well.

I AM GOOD ENOUGH

There's a story dating back to my childhood I forgot to tell but it's so relevant to my "I'm not good enough" belief that I'm going to tell it here. It starts with the annual *Sports Illustrated* swimsuit issue, and, once again, my dad. Sorry, Dad.

It was well-known as I grew up that February was a month to look forward to in our Wisconsin home. While the snow flew liberally outside the window and temps tended to stay in the freezing range, warmth was brought into the house with the annual swimsuit issue of SI. I don't think my dad talked about it constantly, but it was mentioned enough that it made an impact on my impressionable young mind. The swimsuit issue piqued my curiosity as a preteen and one day I actually picked it up out of the magazine rack in the family room to look at it. Inside the pages I found what I guessed was clearly so fascinating to my dad: stunning, scantily-clad young women on beaches around the world. My mom didn't really address the issue with him in front of us (if at all) and she had no idea the effect it was having on my self-image. *Sports Illustrated* was just one more way with which I measured myself "not good enough." My 5'3" 90-lb flat-chested self knew deeply she was not attractive to the eyes of the opposite sex. This is why, in part, I made the dating choices I did during my teen years; I thought I wasn't pretty enough, let alone blessed with boobs enough, to be worthy of a boy's attention. Therefore, when a boy actually appeared to notice me, I felt I'd better do exactly what he wanted in order to keep his eyes on me, even if I knew it was wrong or didn't want to participate.

I did marry a man who well-loved and desired me and my lack of boobs. But no matter how much he told me the size of my breasts did not matter to him, I still felt something lacking inside of me.

When I turned thirty-two Tom had a banner year in sales and he granted my fondest wish: breast implants! I went from a 34-nearly-A to a 34C in a mere few hours and thousands of dollars. I'm not gonna lie: it was the BEST thing I've ever done for myself. Feeling like I was the shape I was "supposed to be" has, for the last 20 years, helped me find the confidence to walk into a room feeling worthy of being part of conversations, getting the job, being heard.

Now, the older I get (and the older my breast implants get) I have emotionally matured enough to know what I saw in the swimsuit issue so long ago was not a realistic representation of women in general. After all, my mom didn't look that way, though I'm not sure why I didn't make that connection at the time. But for years those images have haunted me, made me feel I should just "bounce back" to my best physical self the second after I'd given birth (even though it took months for the pregnancy weight to be gained), and shun all midlife pounds and sag. I felt like I could be the nicest woman in the world but since I didn't have big boobs, forget about it. That's complete bullshit! While I don't want to lose the implants anytime soon, if, God forbid, something happened, at this point in my life I know I am perfectly beautiful and more than good enough without them. Having five kids, the youngest being a daughter in her teens, I have tried to be conscious not to make a big deal of weight, size, or shape and use only positive self-talk around them. And, of course, no Victoria's Secret catalogs grace our home and, even with all the boys in our home, we never subscribed to *Sports Illustrated*.

I AM ABLE TO MAKE HEALTHY CHOICES

Marriage is hard. I made a commitment to love and honor my husband all the days of my life when I was twenty-three years old. Even though I had a kindergartener at the time, I was just a baby myself. And at twenty-five, so was he. Sure, we attended premarital counseling mandated by the Catholic church we were married in, but we only halfheartedly participated because we were deeply in love (and lust). Everything sounded easy then, because love was all we needed, right?

Tom and I marked twenty-nine years of marriage in May of 2021. We have had some serious ups and downs over the years, as all couples do. You can't live with someone day in and day out, through many children, moves, career decisions, and health issues, and not have some challenges.

I would say the first fourteen years of our marriage I lived happily in a la-la land of being the supportive, dutiful wife I was supposed to be. That's what was modeled for me growing up. My parents' divorce in 2006 hit me hard: harder than I thought it would. My parents didn't fight a lot, but I've always been pretty close with my mom. I knew, over the years, they'd had their share of seeing things differently (starting with my pregnancy at eighteen) and they grew apart, until there was really nothing left to save.

My dad has since gone on to remarry, and I am truly happy for him. My mom lives near us and she is equally content on her own, I have never felt otherwise in all the years she's been single. But my parents' split, fourteen years into my own marriage, made me begin to question the probability of a lifelong partner. On the other hand, my in-laws successfully celebrated fifty-plus years of marriage before my father-in-law passed in 2019. From my perspective, as their daughter-in-law who saw them several times a year for decades, they weren't happy with one another all the time. Then again, there is no marriage that is "happy" all the time. However, in their lifetimes they committed to each other, raised four kids together, and impacted more than a dozen grandchildren. They were very social people who seemed to like the same things until the end. From my perspective, they didn't grow apart.

Looking back at when Tom and I got married, love was overflowing for both of us. I know, in retrospect, I was also looking for the security he provided through his work ethic and innate drive to achieve, something I've always deeply admired in him. I also think, for whatever reason, he was looking for someone to "rescue" and take care of. We were the perfect candidates for one another. And we have always worked really well together. But that doesn't mean we always see eye to eye.

I know I've spent some of our years being who he needed me to be rather than who I truly am. And, to be honest, until I began the work of self-development (about the same time Rihanna's tune was popular), I played the part pretty well.

One of the most beautiful and memorable days of our marriage was not the birth of our kids, though each of those were special and memorable, but our twenty-year anniversary. We chose to renew our vows back in Wisconsin among our closest family and friends. We asked each one of the kids to play a part in the ceremony. Nick walked me down the aisle. I asked him to do so not because he is the oldest, but because at our wedding in 1992 he didn't get a say in whether or not I married Tom and it meant a lot to me to have him "give me away." Allen-Michael was already talking about the priesthood so it seemed a natural step to make him the officiant. Brigham did not want to be part of the ceremony, not because he didn't want to see us renew our vows but because he didn't want any attention on him, so he was our videographer. That left a ring bearer and a flower girl; naturally at ages seven and nine, Maddux and Mia were, in my humble opinion, the cutest ever in their roles.

The weather was perfect, the venue was beautiful, and Tom's brother Joe catered the meal, which was absolutely delicious! I knew the day would be special because we were creating and saying our vows in front of those who meant the most to us after twenty years of marriage. But it turned out to be even more deeply meaningful than I thought it could be.

During the last decade of my conscious awakening, I have reflected more on who I am as a wife and how I want to show up for Tom, as well as how I want him to show up for me. Voicing my opinion hasn't always met with agreement because we differ in what we need emotionally and physically from one another. Every day it's a negotiation to be the best we can for each other, knowing we are the living examples of what our children will carry into their own relationships.

At the moment we only have one married kiddo; Nick has been married to a woman who has brought out the best in him for many years. I find it interesting to see our kids grow into adults and navigate the world through the lens of what they were taught in large part by us. I haven't experienced grandparenthood yet but I know when the time is right, I will relish that step in my journey as well. One of the things I am most inspired by as a mom is how vastly different each of the kids is and yet they get along really well in spite of this!

THERE IS ALWAYS ENOUGH

Most of our marriage struggles have revolved around the one thing couples fight about most: money. Our first financial hurdle happened when we moved from Wisconsin to California in 1994. The housing costs were much higher there and, although Tom's new position paid more, it wasn't enough to keep us from trying to figure out how to pay for Christmas the two years we lived there. Though I've worked part-time on and off over the course of our marriage, I always felt the most important place I could be was with our kids. Full-time parenting is not for the weak. To be honest, I don't ever remember us having a discussion about whether or not I'd work. The more kids we had the more difficult it was for me to do anything but be the mom. And, even though I've done a hell of a job (if I do say so myself), this is a priceless but unpaid position.

Another obstacle that sucked us in was feeling as if we had to "keep up" with other couples our age. Having moved so many times we didn't always make money on the sale of our homes and, in 2009, shortly after Nick went to rehab, we actually lost our 5,400 s.f. house to foreclosure and declared bankruptcy because we couldn't sell it in the depressed market.

I actually wanted desperately to move to a smaller home, that much space to upkeep was ridiculous, but I know it took a toll on Tom's ego to have us in that position. We rented several more reasonably-sized homes in the same area until we could buy again in 2014. Now, with only two kids left in it and one of them about to go to college, our house is much more square footage than either of us wants to live in. However, to stay in the same area, we'd have to spend significantly more to downsize.

As mentioned earlier, Tom left corporate America in 2017 to buy a travel franchise because he was tired of working for someone else. Planning vacations for others sounded like much more fun; plus, because we'd always had a really limited travel budget and hadn't gotten to see as much of the world as we'd wanted. That's what was happening before the pandemic. The two of us had been on several cruises, we'd been able to take Maddux and Mia on their first cruise to Alaska, and Tom took Brigham on his first cruise as well. The frustration of having to cancel and rebook dozens of trips for clients and having no income for the past year has been incredibly taxing for Tom mentally and physically. As his main sounding board, it is often difficult for me to witness as well. We both hope he'll be able to weather the pandemic and rebound.

My stepping away from my job at the children's hospital at the end of 2020 has been an outright leap of faith on my part. I believe that the universe is on my side and will support us as I help moms evolve in the way they look at the most important job in their lives: motherhood. I am a "glass half full" kinda girl and now am sure there is always enough. Every day we have a warm home, food on the table, our health, and kids who've been able to roll with COVID is sustenance enough for me to know the world is plentiful.

FINAL THOUGHTS

My intention in sharing my story with you is to plant a seed of becoming more aware of how the beliefs you are living from affect the choices and decisions you make every day. When I work with a client, the very first thing we do is set goals for what they'd like to improve in their relationships with themselves and with their children. When they take the time to invest in themselves and their families, they learn, understand, practice, and make changes in the relationships most important in their lives. As a result, their children can't help but change as well. This doesn't mean every parenting goal they set comes to life exactly as they want it to. We certainly can't control exactly how our children will respond. We have much more control over the personal goals we set for ourselves and in our half of the relationship with anyone else. Helping parents achieve those goals is my passion and, I believe, my purpose. The changes you can make will impact your current relationships and carry over into the next generation so that together we can build a more connected world.

The second issue we address, through an exercise I call *Looking Back to Move Forward*, allows us to revisit childhood experiences long enough to understand why the parenting they are doing today can be negatively impacted by their child(ren)'s words and behaviors. Our core beliefs are triggered by our children's behaviors because they are so important to us. As mentioned in the beginning of the book, we all take on some limiting beliefs about ourselves in childhood. Being triggered can also be, in part, a result of family trauma passed down through our cells. We can't discount the evidence of Dr. Bruce Lipton's work around inheriting some emotional and physical attributes given to us by previous generations.

To illustrate this, I'd like to introduce you to one mom I recently coached. Judy is a mother of three; she has twin daughters who are eight years old and a stepson, Troy, who is sixteen. Judy came to see me because she found herself constantly yelling and feeling highly disrespected by Troy. Troy visits two weekends a month and comes over for dinner once a week; Judy was beginning to dread every moment of his visits.

When Judy and I started working together, she had nothing but complaints about everything from how Troy wouldn't lift a finger around the house to his incessant need to be on his phone 24/7. Jay, Judy's husband and Troy's father, tried to talk with Troy, on occasion, but his behavior did not improve and the conflict was escalating. The tense situation was beginning to affect their marriage and the twins were beginning to give her trouble as well.

Once Judy had her goals in place — to be able to have mutually respectful conversations with Troy, he would pitch in around the house during his stay, and he would spend some time interacting with the family — it was time to look back on her childhood through the *Looking Back to Move Forward* exercise. Through this work, Judy and I uncovered she had not felt seen or heard for most of her childhood. In addition, Judy's mother and father divorced when she was in junior high, her mother remarried, and she never got along well with her stepfather. Judy's mother was orphaned at age six when her mom and dad were killed in a car wreck. The trauma of being left at such a tender age made an impact on Judy's mom and the level to which she was able to nurture Judy while she was growing up. Consequently, this also affected Judy as she parented Troy. You see, we are all connected. The experiences of those who've come before us have an impact; however, we can identify and process these experiences and make conscious choices to do things differently in the future.

Over the weeks we met, Judy came to a deeper understanding of how Troy felt. By becoming a little vulnerable, she was able to have some honest conversations with him and found out Troy hated being called a "visitor" when he was in the home. He didn't feel part of the family and it wasn't his job to make that happen. If we want our kids (and stepkids) to respect us and include us in their lives, we first have to model the behavior for them.

Judy learned many things about parenting during our sessions but, more importantly, she asked herself if it was true she wasn't worth being heard. Intellectually, she knew that wasn't true, but it wasn't until we got it out in the open to question it that she was able to develop a new belief about herself that better served her. Then she could start to live from the belief that what she had to say and how she felt were important. The new belief gave her confidence as a step-parent to Troy and a mom to her twins. She also had to learn the same was true for Troy.

By the time Judy and I wrapped up our coaching relationship, she and Troy had discovered they both enjoyed mountain biking and the family was exploring some nearby trails on the weekends he lived with them. She also helped Troy personalize the guest room so he felt much more like part of the family rather than just a visitor. They still had their difficult moments, but Judy learned to pause and respond rather than react because she was being triggered by Troy's behavior. As a coach, it is so gratifying to help another mother find it in herself to create a healthier, happier, more functional relationship with her children.

The first step to living more authentically from a belief system that serves your highest human self is to look back long enough to acknowledge the limiting beliefs you took on, consciously or unconsciously, and discover how they have affected your life. Once you are aware of those beliefs and their consequences, you cannot become unaware. And every time you say or do something that feeds the limiting belief, you abandon your authentic self. The price becomes too high; I know because I did it for years. You then only have the choice between letting those limiting beliefs continue to control you, or creating and defining new beliefs for yourself and practicing them daily until you live them out naturally. In order to become my authentic self as I raise my children, I have chosen the daily practice of examining my limiting beliefs and replacing them with new beliefs that align with who I truly am.

You can also make this choice. Here are a few questions to reflect on to gauge your readiness:

1) What do I believe about myself?
2) How have my beliefs about myself affected the life I am living?
3) Are my beliefs about myself true and supporting me in living a physically and emotionally healthy life? If not, what isn't true about what I currently believe?
4) Where do my beliefs need to change in order for me to live my best life?
5) Would I benefit from getting the guidance of someone who has done, and continues to do, this work?

It takes courage to change patterns and you are in the driver's seat of the relationship with your children. No, you cannot control them, and if you try and do so you will create power struggles, tension, and disconnection. Instead, you can hold dear the sacred relationship you have with them and come from a place of love which breeds connection. The world needs this more than ever today.

OUR CHILDREN COME THROUGH US, NOT FOR US, EXCEPT FOR THE LESSONS THEY REFLECT TO US [DURING THEIR JOURNEY] IN AN EFFORT TO GROW US UP ALONG THE WAY.

Kim Muench

AUTHOR'S NOTE

My ideal client is one who will see or feel parts of herself within my story and, because of her own parenting journey, has a desire to work on herself in order to create the healthiest, strongest connection with her child(ren). Is this you? Consider this a personal invitation to take the next step and reach out to me. I look forward to working with parents who are ready to reconnect to their inner wisdom, identify and challenge their limiting beliefs, and create new beliefs that better serve the relationship they have with themselves and with those they love most. Peaceful parenting starts with *you* because you are writing the parenting manual your grandchildren will learn from. Conscious/intentional parenting is legacy work and it's the greatest gift we can offer to elevate the future generation.

Please visit my website at www.reallifeparentguide.com or send me an email at reallifeparentguide@gmail.com. I look forward to connecting with you soon!

to go to Kim's website   to go to Kim's YouTube channel

About the Author

Kim Muench is the founder of Real Life Parent Guide and a Jai Institute for Parenting Certified Coach. She is passionate about empowering parents of adolescents to create healthier, happier, more functional relationships with their children. Her home is in Texas but her heart is in building a legacy of strong parenting around the world. Connect with Kim at reallifeparentguide.com.

Made in United States
Troutdale, OR
08/22/2023

12295119R00123